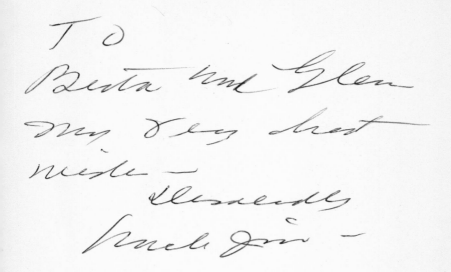

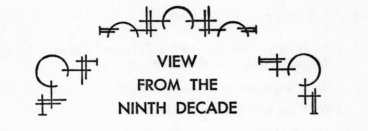

VIEW
FROM THE
NINTH DECADE

BY J. C. PENNEY

J. C. Penney—The Man with a Thousand Partners. An autobiography as told to Robert W. Bruere

Main Street Merchant (in collaboration with Norman Beasley)

Fifty Years with the Golden Rule

Lines of a Layman

VIEW
FROM THE
NINTH DECADE

Jottings from a Merchant's Daybook

by

J. C. PENNEY

THOMAS NELSON & SONS
Edinburgh   NEW YORK   *Toronto*

Published in New York by Thomas Nelson
& Sons and simultaneously in Toronto,
Canada, by Thomas Nelson & Sons (Canada) Ltd.

Library of Congress Catalog Card No.: 60–14121

DESIGNED BY FRANK KARPELES
Manufactured in the United States of America

TO

MY DEVOTED WIFE

Caroline Autenrieth Penney

WHO DEEPLY INSPIRES MY LIFE
THIS BOOK IS
GRATEFULLY DEDICATED

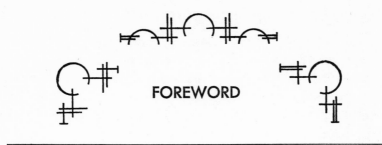

FOREWORD

J. C. Penney is a familiar name to throngs up and down the streets of our towns and cities. Preeminent among merchants, he has built one of the outstandingly successful commercial enterprises of our American economy.

The story of this man's life and achievements reads like a romance, and it is just that. It is a nostalgic, thrilling, up-the-ladder-to-success story in the true American spirit. The son of upright and earnest Christian parents, J. C. Penney was nurtured in the honorable privation of the late frontier. He says of his father that he left only "a good example . . . and two mortgages" to his children. But actually his parents gave J. C. Penney a heritage of faith and character which are obvious and basic in his personality.

Any young person who desires to be a fine success in life will learn much from reading this dynamic book. *View from the Ninth Decade* is filled with practical suggestions on how to do a good job and how to make the most of oneself. It is a gold mine of wise advice from a man who worked to the very top of success and distinction through application of honorable methods all the way.

This life story conclusively shows that the Christian way is not an impractical way. Indeed, it emphasizes the importance and practicality of sound Christian principles in building a creative business career. The Golden Rule is inextricably associated with J. C. Penney. He fearlessly adopted the principle in face of protests and doubters, and against assertions that "it wouldn't work." But he believed that it would work and he held firmly to the principle of the Golden Rule in every activity of his business. And it did work. In fact, it worked gloriously—so well that few businessmen today would question its validity as an effective rule of business practice.

To me Mr. Penney is one of the most lovable and utterly delightful men I have ever known. He has an extraordinary capacity for friendship. Always gracious and kindly he greets everyone with courtly manner. His countenance shows little evidence of the accumulating years. The J. C. Penney, whom we all admire and love so much, comes through in this autobiography.

J. C. Penney has helped and inspired many people. For years he has traveled throughout the United States and in foreign countries speaking to interested audiences everywhere. And he always inspires his listeners to a renewed faith in God. He encourages them to implement their faith by making it the practical core of their personal and business lives. Having shared many public speaking platforms with Mr. Penney, I can testify to the profound impression he makes and to the affection in which he is held by all. His autobiography will prove to be a valuable reading experience.

NORMAN VINCENT PEALE

CONTENTS

VIEW
FROM THE
NINTH DECADE

CHAPTER I

As Though the Impossible Were Possible

Recently I chanced on a statement of sage advice: "Proceed as though the impossible were entirely possible."

It appeals to me as a good rule. For young people, just starting out. For businessmen, with hard problems and decisions to make. For employers and employees, men and women, in trades, professions or whatever working life situation; in fact, for just about anyone who will take its meaning and apply it.

One reason it struck me forcibly is that it brought back feelings of mine when I approached—perhaps it would be more accurate to say when I attacked—my first day in business on my own.

The sign over my store in Kemmerer, Wyoming, that April day in 1902, read *Golden Rule Store.* I do not claim that I was being original. In those days many stores called themselves Golden Rule. Many considered it a slogan of good publicity value. As it happened, the sign meant something rather more important to me, for reasons I will touch on later.

When I got up that first morning, a young man starting out in business for himself in an unfamiliar town, both apprehension and the need to succeed from the first were heavily on my mind. Quite a few people had gone out of their way to caution me. For example, the cashier of the local bank said gravely, "Now you're a young fellow just starting out, and I never like to discourage young people. But I think you ought to know that you won't find it possible to do a cash business here. You see the mining companies around here have stores of their own. They let miners draw coupons against their pay checks; it isn't exactly compulsory but the miners know they're expected to buy from the company store. Incidentally, pretty high prices are charged for things."

Settling in Kemmerer, I hadn't expected it to be easy. I knew I'd have to work very hard. Kemmerer was tiny and struggling, having been settled only a few years. But even if I wanted to, I couldn't afford to extend credit in my store. And there was another reason, a deeper one.

To my mind a storekeeper's first responsibility was to be fair to his customers. A customer-relationship built on credit didn't seem to me fair either to customers or the merchant. A certain number of folks, at least, would buy—or be tempted to—more than they could wisely afford if they didn't have to pay for it right off. Then, when they began casting up what they owed, often they would start to worry, perhaps even before the date for paying the account. Perhaps a child would fall sick during the month, or a father suffer an accident calling for unexpected outlay. It is human nature sometimes for worry to grow into enmity; in the end worry might turn customers against a storekeeper because of having made it possible for them to buy more than they could afford. So it was my idea to avoid from the first anything which might ever raise up a barrier.

I couldn't afford to let the bank cashier's words discourage me; I had too much of an investment at stake, and a wife and baby boy, Roswell, my first-born, to provide for.

Having no idea then, how correct I would turn out to be, I replied, "Mr. Pfeiffer, I believe you may be surprised at what we will do."

He was. So was I. Our first day's business was nearly $500.00 —cash.

We couldn't consider ourselves over the hump. In any town there is a natural tendency for the public to go in and investigate any new store. Late that night I asked myself: when the novelty wears off, will enthusiasm for our values and way of doing business hold up? It is a very important point, that when parcels are opened at home, values must prove as good as they looked to be at the time of purchase. Only confidence, and knowing how they can expect to be treated, will bring customers back a second time, and keep them coming back. This was the way of doing business for which I wanted to be known. It is important anywhere, at any time; it was all the more important at that particular time in Kemmerer, where the population was only 1,000—and there were twenty-one saloons which were glad to accept company coupons as legal tender.

My sign was important to me personally, therefore, because it was intended to be taken at face value. *The best goods for the least money* was our tangible expression of the Golden Rule. Combined with training along these lines by businessmen whose example I admired, it also stemmed instinctively from early home influences, and principles instilled in us from childhood by our parents. I never heard either of them use the term *Golden Rule;* it simply exemplified the spirit of their everyday way of doing things.

More important at the close of that first business day than having confounded the bank cashier's solemn prediction was the evidence that, in a hard competitive world, principle adapted to business practice will work. Nowadays one hears considerable about the necessity for using "gimmicks" if one wants to do business successfully. I believe that principles, sincerely applied, will work a magic which gimmicks never can.

I have been looking through daybook jottings from the perspective of my ninth decade, and from having spent nearly sixty years as a merchant. The Penney Company corporate story is fairly well known and as such does not need repeating here. In culling certain observations about business and less known personal experiences to include in this little book, I am reminded over and over that no turn of business conditions, no changing times ever furnished any good reason to put expediency in place of the principles which determined our business rules at the outset. First and foremost was that great principle for all just human dealings, which has come down to us from the Sermon on the Mount.

I travel a good many thousands of miles around the country each year, helping to open new stores, looking in on the growth and progress of older ones. Often I am invited to speak before civic, youth, fraternal, religious and other audiences, and I meet a great many people in various walks of life. I receive and answer a heavy daily mail. Though it is the range of subject matter which interests me more than the number of letters received and sent, my Executive Assistant—who, I must say, has a livelier taste for records than I do—says that I write an average of four hundred answering letters a month. From my combined activities I get encouragingly definite signs of an increase in the positive application to everyday affairs of the Golden Rule. To cite one example, recently I noticed reference in a newspaper to the National Association of Real Estate Boards, and that Realtor-members subscribe to a decalogue including, among its six clauses, "I pledge myself to act fairly towards all, in the spirit of the Golden Rule."

There is an axiom, that in order to get rid of an evil its cause must be understood. I never see much use in bewailing what is wrong with the world and the times, unless we are willing to understand causes, and individually do something positive toward removing evils. I agree with Billy Graham, who reminds his hearers repeatedly, "The hearts of men must change before the world can be changed." What universal rivers of peace and practical good can flow over the world and humankind when people in great numbers find it worth their while to make the Golden Rule work; make it as much an everyday personal tool as a typewriter, a telephone, a plow, a truck. It will not always be easy, but it will be possible when we make it so. In this connection I am reminded that the great evangelist D. L. Moody used to urge people, "Don't pray for easy lives! Pray to be stronger men!"

When I was ten there was a big revival at the Hamilton Baptist Church. I thought I wanted to join the church and —though my father was of the Old School Baptist persuasion and this church in Hamilton was Missionary Baptist—I spoke to him about it. He questioned me rather closely, asking whether I thought I was ready to take such a serious step.

I decided that perhaps I might not be ready, and dropped the matter. But I had entered a phase which many boys experience. I felt full of vague religious stirrings and—with my father's calling as a preacher constantly before me—moved by seeing him suffer greatly for his principles, I decided I wanted to become a preacher. I began carrying a Bible with me wherever I went. Even the Biblical "two or three, gathered together" were hardly needed for me to launch out into a "sermon." Ultimately I subdued my ambition for the ministry though I retain the habit of always taking a Bible with me when I travel.

I would not like, however, to give any impression of preaching in this book. If I feel tempted—all of us are, at one time or another—to sermonize a bit about personal experiences and the lessons of life, I remind myself of a schoolboy I once heard about, and a theme he wrote for a class in English. It was short and to the point:

> Socrates was a Greek philosopher. He told everyone what to do. He got poisoned.

That, it seems to me, ought to be warning enough to anyone, not to impose experience, which, in any case, is best only shared.

CHAPTER II

"Train Up the Young. . . ."

A letter came to me from a woman in one of the Mountain states. She began by saying she'd never seen me, and did not expect she ever would, but that in a way she felt she knew me, having traded in one of the Penney stores for over forty years. Her letter was written in a simple, neighborly way that made it sound as though she were just talking across the counter while I showed her pillowcases, dish towels and winter stockings for the children.

She recalled hearing many years ago that our Company had been founded on the Golden Rule principle. "Must be that you got that from your folks when you were young," she wrote. "It would be better if more parents took time today to teach it to their young folks, put it good and deep into their minds, to go by all their lives. I just seemed to have the idea the Golden Rule could cure some of this juvenile delinquency; come to think of it, maybe some grown-up delinquency too. Anyway, I thought I'd just let you hear I'm glad you pay attention to the Golden Rule in business."

I find pleasure in replying to such letters. I wouldn't want it to seem that I think of myself as unique in relating Golden Rule practice in business. At the time I started out many other men were doing likewise; the example of my parents, and the practice of several men I worked for after I got out of high school influenced me in making it a positive part of my personal business policy. Today I am but one of thousands upon thousands doing so. I am often impressed by the variety of ways in which businessmen relate themselves openly to Golden Rule practice. For example, the other day one of our retired Penney store managers sent me an uncommonly handsome little booklet he had received at Christmas time from a friend in the business community, a motor car distributor. The booklet is titled *The Golden Rule* and illuminated in the style of medieval manuscripts by Carl A. Mundstock. The text, accompanied by illuminations embodying designs and symbols associated with each, presents the Golden Rule in the forms in which it appears in seven great religions. The businessman had added his own message to his friends as follows: "It's Christmas! At this season it is well to remind ourselves that all of us would be living in a better world if we went beyond knowing the Golden Rule, and tried to live by it." This is but one bit of the evidence I see on all sides, that people are turning to this great principle as about the only way left for this distressed old world.

We used to hear it said more years ago than nowadays, I think, "Train up a child in the way he should go, and when he is old he will not depart from it." I covet for young people everywhere a return to the kind of parental example and gui-

dance I knew in my boyhood home. Especially from the time
I went into business on my own, no day of my life but has
felt the influence of their precepts and attitudes. Broadly
speaking, I can say, that when I stayed close to them, things
went well; when I became neglectful, I got into trouble. Pres-
ently I will relate an instance of the latter.

Because of this pervasive effect on my life of parental example, I should like the reader to understand a little about them,
and the life of our home which has been of such value all
through my personal and business life. Nowadays many parents are deeply concerned over "what to do about" their children. They feel that if they are too strict, the young people
may rebel—perhaps rebel into really serious trouble. They feel
that if parents are too lenient about values and principles,
that, too, may invite trouble.

At this distance it seems to me that my parents were neither
too strict nor too lenient, but just right. Lest it be thought that
I must have been just too good a boy for this earth, there were
many times when I thought darkly that they were hard and
unfeeling; but then, it is ever the way of the young and growing, to feel put-upon! The proof—that they were thinking always of what was best for me—must be that the ideals and ideas
they instilled have stayed with me, seeming as natural a way of
life for me as it did for them. Their lives were never, never
easy, yet that never afforded any excuse for compromise. At
times it cost them dearly to hold fast to their beliefs, and in
boyhood years this cost me periods of great bitterness.

Among autobiographies of men who have lived interesting
and productive lives, I frequently notice a common denominator. Many a father of such men worked a farm during the
week, and served on the Sabbath as preacher to some small,

rural flock. Seemingly the aftermath of the war—economic uncertainty, moral and spiritual anxiety, perhaps a subconscious feeling of lingering social guilt—stirred people to a new need to hear the eternal truths reaffirmed. As settlement fanned out, log churches sprang up and there weren't enough ordained ministers to serve all; and so men, though unordained, whose convictions were deep, filled in the gaps, preaching out of deep faith the saving grace of Christ and the infinite mercy of God. My father, James Cash Penney, was such a man.

When he came home to Missouri in 1865 after the war, he bought a tract of three hundred and ninety acres—mostly raw prairieland—from the railroad; down in one corner a small bituminous coal mine was later discovered which he leased out to a mining company at a royalty of five cents a ton.

Weekdays he worked the farm and bought cattle, grazing them and sending them to market. Over in Kentucky he married a Kentucky-born cousin, Mary Frances Paxton, and took her back to Missouri whither his father, a minister and also Kentucky-born, the Reverend Eli Penney, had migrated years earlier.

My mother had grown up in the sheltered life of a well-to-do home and received convent-school education—not because the Paxtons were Roman Catholics, which they were not—but because the nuns were skilled in teaching.

So life in the raw, undeveloped region of Hamilton and the farm was a great change for her. She demonstrated her quality, cheerfully and with self-sacrificing courage, by doing the work of three women and raising a large family; twelve children in all, six living to adulthood; and by holding up her husband's hands also, in his labors as preacher to a Primitive Baptist congregation some dozen miles distant from Hamilton, at Log Creek.

In our home we were never hungry, never cold, but we were certainly poor. Without ever debating the point, our parents demonstrated that rich values are to be had which are not bought with money. My father had been graduated from college—Pleasant Ridge College, near Weston in Platt County on the Kansas border—at the age of seventeen. Ironically this later militated against him; even so it sustained his love of books and belief in education.

My parents had a deep concern for education for their children. They were staunch believers in the importance of learning discipline early and the classic belief of the young, that school teachers are natural enemies, received no encouragement from them; it was well understood that if I received a rattaning in school I could expect another at home.

We had subscriptions to the local weekly newspaper, besides *The Youth's Companion,* and *St. Nicholas,* and current events always came up for discussion in the evenings. My father considered debating interesting in itself and good training for the mind; proposing a subject, he would give me my choice, affirmative or negative; whichever I took, I usually wound up looking like a simpleton because he could feint and thrust with the ease and grace of a fencer, but I didn't mind too much because he managed to make even losing interesting.

We were expected to be well acquainted with the Bible and to commit a good representation of Bible verses to memory, which we did without serious objection. He had a knack for relating the everyday life of the household and farm to places and incidents in the Bible. I was inclined to be impatient when things did not go fast enough to suit me; smiling indulgently, on such occasions he was apt to quote to me from Scripture. "You know, the Bible tells us 'Be patient therefore, brethren, unto the coming of the Lord. Behold, the husbandman waiteth for the precious fruit of the earth and hath long patience for it, until it receive the early and latter rain.' After supper tonight you might look that up in the New Testament; it's in the Book of James, fifth chapter, I believe." Once when I rebelled against its taking such a long time to be considered old enough to do something on which I had set my heart, he said perhaps I might feel a bit better about it if I read over the third chapter of Ecclesiastes. "It begins 'To every thing there is a season, and a time to every purpose under the sun.' If you think about it, you'll know there's sense to God's plans for our development. When the time's right you'll be able to do this thing you're so set on."

Family life then was much more closely knit than the average nowadays. As I look about at the outside interests available to teenagers now, it doesn't seem to me that we were so badly off, even though our outside pleasures and distractions were fewer and of the simplest kind. I remember home as a little world in itself, self-contained and dependable, graced by the buoyant love and sunny disposition of our mother, and made gravely genial and reassuring by the constant concern and guiding mind of our father. Church and Sunday School were fixed activities. In summer we swam and fished with our companions, skated in winter on a pond at the Fair Grounds, had other traditional places to visit at stated times of the year, such as the County Fair, where a lot was to be seen and enjoyed without its costing too much, or an occasional performance by a traveling minstrel troupe at the Odd Fellows or Grange Hall. If you were early in line, more than likely you could earn a ticket of admission by distributing handbills for the management. Once a year a circus might come through, too, maybe even Forepaughs' big one.

My father's great concern for his children included our being self-reliant. I was eight years old when he initiated my training in that direction by letting me know that I would have to find the way to buy my own clothing, then and for the future. It came as an awful shock, at a time when I had been savoring several things I would buy with $2.50 I had earned laboriously, working in the hayfield. To make matters worse, I suddenly remembered that there was quite a hole in the sole of one of my only pair of shoes. He couldn't mean that I must begin right off to buy my own clothes—he couldn't —— In the golden light of the kerosene lamp my eyes besought him as I asked if he wouldn't buy me just this one more pair of shoes.

"No, Jim, I won't be able to do that. It's time you got to learning to depend on yourself. As soon as you get the hang of it, I wouldn't wonder if you'll feel quite proud, buying whatever you need out of your own money."

Maybe so, but it certainly seemed unlikely; I felt stupefied.

I went to bed feeling utterly cast off, and by my own father! I knew very well that he was interested in my good, so there must be something there somewhere which was right. But I was too young, this was too hard, too hard. It took all the starch out of me.

A boy's way is to sleep sound, like a fox in a hole, and I dozed off, exhausted. But soon I waked up, tossing and turning. A dead stillness lay over the house. Nobody cared how miserable I was! Straggling across the footboard of my bed, figures mocked me. $2.50 . . . $2.50 . . . Who's going to buy his own new pair of shoes now? $2.50. . . . I lunged about the bed, thinking despairingly, "There goes that jack-knife I've saved up for . . . There goes the copy of James Fenimore Cooper's *The Last of the Mohicans* . . ." In school I hated reading; if you stumbled over a word everybody snickered. Spelling was different, though. I liked spelling bees and didn't even mind that you had to "tow the mark"; if your foot happened to slip over the chalk mark on the wooden floor, the next in line got your chance at the word. But I liked reading when I was by myself, and had been planning a long time to buy Cooper's book.

In my misery I cried a little. A night bird passed over the house, crying along mournfully with me. I went back to sleep, like any healthy growing boy.

A boy believes such tragedies will surely kill him and for a time wishes they would. As days passed I wished so less and less. One day I could look at Pa's decision without rage and despair. I bought a new pair of shoes. The sales clerk seemed to think it was some kind of joke when he saw me count the money out of my battered purse. I gave him the cold stare of a mature man not to be trifled with, and he hurried away to wrap my parcel.

I was taken out of myself sharply by an experience which befell our parents. It had to do with my father's ministry and seemed to me about the worst treatment I had ever heard of for a man who never neglected his duty, winter or summer, freezing snow or torrential rain, whether he felt ill or well.

By nature a liberal thinker, circumstances caused Father to take a firm stand for three matters, frowned on rather widely at that time, He advocated men being educated for the ministry. He wanted them paid stipends for their labors. He came out strongly on the side of Sunday Schools; having managed the attendance of his own children at Sunday School, that would have been enough to satisfy most men. But he was the kind of man who wanted all young people to enjoy advantages equally.

We have come a long way from times when critics frankly feared Sunday School as "inviting the hoodwinking of children, and attempts to teach the doctrines of the Trinity, and Atonement." But our father was called up on charges and, by decision of the majority, read out of his church. It was implied benignly that Mother could remain.

They didn't know Mother. She stood up and declared calmly, "I believe as my husband believes. If you read Jimmy out, you must include me." It was very embarrassing to the authorities but they saw they could not change her.

I felt overwhelmed with bitterness in the face of such injustice and went around declaring that there was no God, at times even saying so out loud. Gradually, however, the forbearance of my parents, their tranquil refusal to allow the episode to embitter them or affect their faith and trust in God, worked to make me let go my own hold on anger and bitterness.

The fact that Father was strict and, from the viewpoint of a growing boy, quite unbending sometimes, could not becloud my fierce loyalty to him. At times I found rather sharp ways of expressing it.

A longtime Democrat, when he joined the Populist Party and decided to run for Congress on its ticket, he was sometimes called on to explain. He would say that it was not he who had left the Democrat Party but the Democrat Party which had left him, on issues which he deemed for the good of the country, including Free Silver.

In a campaign rally he was attacked rudely by an opponent. One thing the man said was all the more awful to me because he, like Father, was a minister of the Gospel! It happened that this gentleman was cross-eyed, which certainly was not his fault but did give him a somewhat warlike expression. He was quite a formidable figure, always wearing a Prince Albert coat.

"James Cash Penney hasn't got even a string for a backbone!" the man roared, in the glare of the kerosene torches. I could hardly believe my ears. My father, with no backbone?

I waited until the man finished and was leaving the scene of the rally. Pushing past those accompanying him, I seized him by the skirts of his frock coat and yanked. He turned sharply. Seeing it was only a spindly youth—a convert to the cause, no doubt—he bestowed on me his best political smile. But when I cried loudly, "What you said about my father is a lie! You lied! You lied!" the smile vanished, leaving a stunned expression. A few bystanders laughed heartily; a couple of cohorts pushed me to one side; the candidate stared at me coldly and turned away; the incident was over. I had no doubt I would be reprimanded when my father heard I had publicly called a man a liar. But what mattered most? Being polite, or standing up for your father?

He did hear about it. Instead of reproving me he mused, quietly, "Jim, you remember, in the Bible, where it says we are to love our enemies, bless them that curse us, pray for them that despitefully use us?" He didn't say anything further. He didn't have to. It drove home even harder his example of forbearance in the incident of being turned out of his church.

I couldn't forgive and forget so easily. Moving along in my formative years, I often asked myself why such good and unselfish people as my parents should have so many trials. They received so little in the way of material ease, so little respite from hard-pressed labor. Yet I would not have the reader think our family life was nothing but hard work, deprivation and sacrifice. Year in and year out we certainly did have about as little ready cash as would be possible and still got along. Yet in that we were not greatly different from the general run of farming families. And we had things to be thankful for; the fruits of the land, enough small pleasures to go on, and other, less tangible, things which were not bought with money. The kitchen was the hub of the family's life, and certainly the very opposite of a picture of hardship. Interesting talk, a prevailing cheerfulness, mutual consideration and quiet affection eddied all around, blessing everything including the piles of freshly washed and ironed clothing and linens, the simmering kettle of hearty soup stock on the back of the woodstove, the apple pie, rich with cinnamon and nutmeg, baking in the oven. Times were tight, all right, but no more so for us than for others; and my father, greatly interested in the social conscience and philosophy of an inspiring thinker named Henry George, never let us lose hope that a turn for the better would come. He went along calmly, doing his best for his family as he saw it, taking pleasure in opening our eyes to the world about us. He kept close track of current events, new inventions and other topics of broad interest.

Though not given to easy joking, he and Mother both had a knack for humorous sidelights on subjects that came up in family talk. He was very interested when one of those new things called an automobile was exhibited in 1889 at the Paris Exposition—he read that it was a Benz—and commented dryly that it put him in mind of John Fitch's steamboat demonstrations, and of the farmer, watching from the riverbank, who said, flatly, "Well, now they've got the thing started, they'll never be able to stop it."

Partly because he had benefitted from it, partly too because college education was an advantage he thought all would do well to aspire to, even though it might be beyond the reach of one's pocketbook, he often discussed the subject. Not everyone in those days looked on it as desirable, and Mother was fond of telling about a minister she had known in Kentucky. A man well up in years, he often took satisfaction in informing people, "Thank God my shoulders have never brushed a college wall!"

Thinking of the diligence with which we try to make more leisure time today, I have the feeling that we appreciated more the little we had then. An excursion could only be taken after the most rigid saving and careful planning. At Fourth of July every firecracker had to go off. Unless we could find some job connected with it, entertainment which cost any money was out of the question. When I was invited to come and visit for a few days with an aunt and uncle living forty-nine miles away, in St. Joe, it was a real event. We could get in a bit of fishing in Lake Contrary, and a bit of sightseeing. We visited the stables of the famed pony express, and vicariously experienced a scary tingle in a quiet St. Joe side street, walking past the prosaic frame dwelling which had been the home of the wild James boys. Jesse had died back in 1882, but we imagined the house as still wreathed in mists of dark doings.

My aunt and uncle had one living child whom, not unreasonably, they wished to continue living. This boy, somewhat fragile and timid, played during my visits in rather gingerly fashion, not in the least enthusiastic about my more energetic ways. When it was time for me to return home my aunt —by nature one to speak the flat truth, no matter what— would tell me with rueful frankness, "Jim, I always enjoy seeing you come; but I declare, I enjoy seeing you go, too. I always seem to feel afraid that you'll manage to break your cousin Leon's neck for him."

When I was about fourteen, my father took me along with him on a trip to Chicago which I have remembered in many connections in the years since. He had grazed and fattened cattle for market, and had a trainload on this occasion. A certain number of carloads entitled the shipper to take a couple of helpers along; on this trip he took my brother-in-law and me. We rode in the caboose; throughout the journey the talk of the trainmen was lively and colorful, at times pungent, always interesting to a boy; traveling into outer space today could be no more so.

We had a little time to spare in the metropolis, so Father took me to see the Board of Trade. He pointed out a man sitting in the center of the room; though a big hubbub boiled all around him he sat perfectly still in his hard chair, absolutely unperturbed. He wore a big overcoat and a black felt plantation hat pulled well forward, putting a good deal of his face in shadow. It struck me as remarkable that this man, looking so aloof from the noisy scene, was nevertheless trading tremendous amounts in wheat. "Everybody calls him Old Hutch," Father said, adding that at one time he had cornered the wheat market. After I got out in the world on my own, whenever I heard mention of a commodity market being cornered, I recalled that hunched-over figure in the hard chair, one hand clasped over the other on the head of a blackthorn cane between his knees, sitting motionless and expressionless while fortunes were traded noisily around him.

I was an indifferent student in school, a fact which later on was to have both bad and good effect. The main reason I never came within even shooting distance of head of the class was that, having to provide for my own clothing needs, it was too important to me to be planning how to make a dime—and then how to make another dime. In hard ways I learned that even the smallest necessaries cost money. A quarter-of-a-dollar was very hard indeed to accumulate, and as for a dollar —I had to rack my brain even to think up ways to earn three cents or a nickel. I read stories about the 49-ers, seeking gold in the forbidding mountain ranges, and it was said that the ones who sought God along with seeking gold were the ones who were most successful. Like most growing boys I had times of doubt about God and religion, and wanted to be provided with proof. Considering my difficulties in making just dimes and quarters, it seemed to me that this association of God and the 49-ers must be an exaggeration. Though I was growing fast, I did not yet grasp that adults are made from boyhood by time and the experiences that come with time.

To earn money I collected horseshoe nails from the blacksmith's floor, ran errands, cut grass, drove cows to pasture, delivered packages, fetched and carried for the ladies when there was a church supper or rummage sale. The Penneys never had to go on the town charity list but it was well known in Hamilton that we, like many others, had to make-do with little money. Still, when I cut a neighbor woman's grass and she tried to pay me off in cookies instead of the agreed fifteen cents, I explained distantly that we had a cookie jar at home and that it was never empty, absolutely never. Blushing, she paid me the agreed fifteen cents but with a sniff, as though letting me know that it might be just as well if I looked elsewhere for grass to cut.

The time came when it seemed to me that nearly everyone wanted to know what I was going to be. I felt nervous and irritable because I couldn't settle my mind on anything I wanted to be. I thought I would be interested in the law, but that was out of the question, it seemed; it would require a college education and my parents couldn't possibly spare tuition even to get me started; besides, probably I wouldn't be able to meet the requirements, not having made the most of the schooling I had.

I worked in a grocery store and thought I might like to be a grocer but the idea was cut short by an incident of which my father made full use to drive home a lesson in integrity.

In the evenings we were encouraged to recount happenings of the day which had interested us. One night at the supper table I happened to tell of something I had observed in the store. In describing it I picked out the word "foxy" to characterize the grocer. It proved to be an unfortunate choice.

The grocer stocked two grades of coffee. One, a well-known popular brand of package coffee, sold for fifteen cents to twenty cents a pound. A mocha-java blend sold for forty cents. I noticed that the grocer poured quite an amount of the package grade into the mocha-java cannister, and sold the result at forty cents.

Father listened with a strange expression. I laughed at the cunning of the grocer, and Father frowned heavily. "Is that all you see in this, Jim, that the grocer is foxy?"

I was startled. "Well, I—" One glance told me he was very disappointed in me.

"Tell me," he said, "if the grocer found someone palming off an inferior article on him for the price of the best, do you think he would think that they were just being foxy, and laugh about it?"

"I guess not—I guess I just didn't think about it that way."

"No, Jim, I guess you just didn't think. Well, do so now, and learn something from it. Another thing. Tomorrow you go to your employer, collect whatever money's due you, and say you won't be working there any longer."

I was flabbergasted. In Hamilton jobs weren't so plentiful that you could afford to just throw one away. But I knew I must do as he said. Honestly and integrity came first. A number of times I heard Father say, "When I'm gone, if people passing my grave can say 'Here lies all that is mortal of an honest man' I couldn't ask for anything better; it's the finest thing a man can have remembered about him."

Throughout late 1894 and early 1895 all the family noticed how poorly Father was feeling. He didn't complain; there was nothing specific; he just seemed all tired out, low in spirits, and without his customary vigor and optimistic interest. We thought the weather might have something to do with it; when it changed, he would pick up again.

The year turned; 1895 settled down for that long, hard pull when it seems that Spring never will come. From our house the flat town stretched out, an etching in bleakness; black, gray, white. The ground showed patches of black soil tufted here and there with white snow. Tree trunks were skeletal; black, steel gray, silver. Leafless branches were a black lace; lilac, maple, box-elder, elm.

"Jim," Father said slowly to me one day, staring out the window at nothing, "I just don't see what's going to become of you; the land's all been taken up." When he'd bought his land he'd paid $9 an acre; since then land had gone to $100 an acre and all had been snapped up. My sister Mittie and my brother Elie had their own farms. Father was taking it for granted that when the time came I'd want to follow them into farming. He was always thinking ahead for his children, and what worried him was where I'd find land.

This was not the time to speak of it, I knew, but I was sure I would never want to just settle down to farming, whatever became of me. Cattle were bringing three or four cents on the hoof, hogs the same; eggs were ten cents a dozen, corn ten cents a bushel. I hadn't been anything extra at school in arithmetic but I could see little promise for me in farming. When I had to I could plow a furrow, had done it often enough, but there was a lot of uncertainty to farming. In the early days much of Father's land was sowed to wheat; there were no reapers and binders, so he cradled; often he was plagued by wet weather, and a shortage of hands at harvest time. I couldn't say so to Father, but somehow land and I never seemed to have anything to say to each other. And I was ambitious, even though I still had nothing definite in mind.

I respected and loved my parents, wanted to please them

and make them proud of me. In those days piracy in business
was far from unknown. Father often said that it wasn't possible for a man to make a million and still remain a Christian.
My parents had made me a Christian but I wanted also to be
a success and become wealthy. I was sure I'd never do it by
farming.

That January day in 1895 the talk with my father dwindled
away on a question mark. "What's going to become of you,
Jim?" The subject was dropped and I was relieved; I had
nothing to tell him that would ease his mind.

Never saying to me in so many words, "I can see that you
don't take to farming, so we'll just see if I can help you get
started in some other line," a few days later he forced his
waning strength to the extent of paying a call on the leading
merchants in Hamilton. Two brothers, the Hales, owned a
drygoods store; it stood out in the community, for the reputation of the proprietors and the excellence of their merchandise.

It was drawing on to February. At that season of the year
businessmen were not interested in taking on new help.

Father didn't say, "Will you give my boy a job? What will
you pay him, and what are the hours?" He said, "Mr. Hale,
I'd like you to take my boy and teach him the fundamentals
of honest business."

"Well, Mr. Penney," Mr. Hale said, "we aren't taking on
any new help at this time of year."

"When Jim likes a thing he works hard at it. I've noticed
he takes to selling," Father must have said. He did not go
into details about my taste for selling; on several occasions,
involving such commodities as pigs and watermelons, circumstances had brought sharp disagreement between us.

Mr. Hale agreed to hire me for the balance of the year.

"But I'll only be able to pay him $25.00 for the eleven months," he explained.

"Jim will profit more in experience than money," Father said, and the matter was settled.

I didn't exactly jump at the prospect. Two dollars and twenty-seven cents a month! I could drive a delivery wagon and get $25.00 a month. On the other hand, what could you learn by driving a wagon?

With conflicting feelings I started working for the Hales. Though I had been keeping myself in clothes almost ten years, I still had neither the money, nor the sense of goods and fit, to dress well; I made myself neat and clean but by comparison with the other clerks I knew painfully that I cut rather a queer figure. In turn this made me clumsy and uncertain about stepping forward with alacrity to wait on customers. I soon discerned that, when the Hales were not around to see, other clerks made a sort of campaign of steering customers away from that greenhorn, Jim Penney, and it was considered a good joke. This confused and angered me and I made many mistakes. It was no comfort to me that Abraham Lincoln said, "A man who can't make mistakes can't make anything." My sales were poor. The experienced clerks were allowed to cut prices if necessary to make sales, but I was told I must get the prices marked for merchandise. The customers were shrewd and those who bargained hardest got what they wanted at their own price. When easing customers away from me was too evident, clerks would say, laughing, "Mr. Hale is afraid you'll lose the sale," but they knew that part of my falling behind on sales was because I couldn't cut prices. I told myself the Hales wouldn't keep me for even the eleven months.

Nevertheless, I was learning. One of the first things Mr. Hale taught me was "never turn your back on the front door." Even when you were waiting on a customer it grew habit to catch the eye of the customer coming into the store and say, "I'll be with you in just a few minutes."

Discouraged as I often felt, the prospect of being let go by the Hales would affect me like a dousing in ice water. I commenced to see that—instead of squaring off against the odds and beating them—I was making excuses for myself. I read a good deal, particularly stories of adventure in tight places, and biographies of men who stood up to tremendous disadvantages and won out. I don't believe I knew at that time about Emerson's thought: "We are parlor soldiers. We shun the rugged battles of Fate, where strength is born." But I was much impressed by what Marshall Field accomplished, after a start which, to say the least, was unpromising. For five years he had been apprenticed to the keeper of a general store at Pittsfield in the Berkshire Hills region of Massachusetts, who finally minced no words in telling young Field's father to get him in some other line of business because he certainly wasn't cut out for being a merchant. It made the young man very angry and he vowed to show his father, his former employer, and everyone else! Which, as all the world came to see, he did.

Like Marshall Field I became very angry, not at anyone else, however, but at my own lack of progress. As though it were yesterday I can recall stepping to the rear of the store, standing there behind a counter, pounding my fist and declaring wrathfully, "They're not going to stop me! They're not! I'll show them——"

A different employee went back on the floor to wait on customers. I stopped listening to jibes and began seeing to it that I got my fair share of customers. I "faced the front door at all times" and sold merchandise. It must have given the Hales some confidence in me for, before long, they permitted me to use my judgment about prices. Although I don't remember hearing any talk on the ground of its being unethical, I never liked shading prices. To me it was not only unethical but poor practical policy too. This was amply proven one hot summer afternoon at a picnic of local farmers. Two men turned up wearing identical suits bought at Hales. It came out speedily that each man had paid a different price. It took the one who had paid the regular price quite a while to get over his grudge.

By the end of the eleven months I was third in sales among seven clerks. The Hales said, "Don't worry about our letting you go, Jim; in fact, next year your salary will be $200.00 instead of $25.00."

One March evening, when I had been with the Hales only a few weeks, my father called us around his bedside. He always had enjoyed talking with his family when the day's work was done, but this evening was different. We hardly admitted it to ourselves, but we knew he was dying. It was as though he were a shepherd, counting his flock over quietly before he must hand it over to other care.

He went around the little family circle, one by one; a word of commendation here, a bit of advice there, and quiet encouragement. Our mother sat in a chair nearby. A slight, trust-

ing smile covered up her foreboding and distress, though I
noticed a trembling of her hands, tightly clasped under her
crisp apron of blue gingham.

Father's tired eyes came to rest on me. During these last
weeks he had been watching how I took hold of the job. I
wouldn't worry him by letting him know the disappointments
which, to him, would only mean anyway that I had to try
harder.

His gaze held mine. He smiled a little. "Jim's going to make
it," he said, glancing around among the others. "I like the
way he started out."

Oncoming Spring was beginning to show itself in tiny dots
of green on sapling branches, in the infinitesimal unrolling
of the intricately folded new leaves on the shrubs, forsythia,
and syringa, and the firebush. But with the change of weather
he didn't pick up.

When he died it was hard to believe. He had always been
so alive, like the sturdiest oak.

It was said freely in the town that James Cash Penney left
everything he had to his family: his blessing, his good example, and two mortgages.

They didn't mention the legacy he left me, I suppose because they didn't know about it. "Jim will make it," he had
said. That was my legacy. Those words gave me my goal.

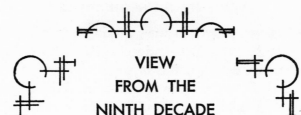

VIEW
FROM THE
NINTH DECADE

CHAPTER III

The Spirit of Service Must Be the Center

I was nearing twenty when my father died; there was nothing yet to show that I would not continue, for some time at least, in my home town. The opportunities were limited but I still had no clear idea where to look for larger ones. I had begun to hit my stride with the Hale brothers and, like the general run of young men at that age, I went along from day to day. Though my third decade opened under the shadow of my father's passing and the inevitable efforts of the family to adjust to the hard disruption, for my part there were the encouraging signs that I had settled into work for which I was suited and which suited me, in that it called forth a zest for putting into it that extra effort which makes the difference between the routine and the constructive. In the course of being thwarted at salesmanship, out of angry desperation I had buried myself in learning stock, keeping it neatly arranged, clean and inviting to the eye, methodically placing it

on counters and shelves in ways making it possible for customers to be served quickly and well. I trained myself to observe customers, noting points of store service which pleased
or displeased them. Being no longer vulnerable, fellow clerks
lost interest in using me as an object of torment. Probably I
wouldn't have agreed that I was ready to settle down in Hamilton for life, but I certainly had no plans to seek larger fields.

With terrible suddenness the choice was taken out of my
hands. What seemed nothing more than a persistent bronchial
cold caused the family doctor to say firmly, "Jim, I want you
to get to a different climate, dryer. Do it right away. I would
advise Denver. And another thing; you must not work inside."
I was too shocked for it to appear even remotely possible that
it would all work as a blessing in disguise.

In the two years since Father's death the farm had done well.
I often think the stand taken by Mother had a lot to do with
it. Being the sort of woman she was, she could take no other.
Naturally, well-meaning people offered an abundance of free
advice, and most of it centered around the idea that, inasmuch as there were two mortgages, she should give up the un-
equal burden and let the farm go. She would not turn her back
on honest debts and said she guessed she'd manage somehow.
In the end every dime owed was paid.

Nature itself seemed to come to her aid. In his last year
Father had been persuaded to plow up a considerable acreage
of his bluegrass pastureland and plant to corn. A yield of
18,000 bushels brought twenty-five cents a bushel, making a
good start on paying off the mortgages.

To show for two years from the time of Father's death to

the day when the doctor gave his opinion, I had a bit more than $300 in savings. Keeping out just enough for traveling to Denver and room and board until I found work, I left the $300 behind with Mother. She fixed me a cardboard box of food for the journey—a whole roast chicken, sandwiches, pears and apples, a loaf of brown bread—and I set off. It was the depth of a very hot summer; drinking water, sloshing in the tank at the end of the railroad coach, was not very refreshing.

After a day and night the air cooled. When I got down with my heavy valise at Denver I felt a tingle of adventure and anticipation.

Confidently mentioning my store experience with the Hales, I got a job, at $6.00 a week. Taking time only to locate room and board at $4.50 a week, I went to work, this time better able to stand off attempts by other clerks to snatch customers from someone evidently regarded as an eastern tenderfoot. Within a few weeks I decided I could better myself and found another job. Almost at once I ran into the two-price system. "If you can't sell those socks in the 25¢-a-pair box," the proprietor ordered, "sell those in the 2-for-a-quarter box; the point is, sell socks." The socks were the same in both boxes. I didn't like the idea of the two prices. "But that isn't honest!" I objected.

"Sell socks, don't give me your opinion!" my employer cried. I knew well enough what Father's advice would be if he were alive. I collected my wages and left the job. It was a wrench; I wanted to sell drygoods and the number of drygoods stores was limited in Denver. However, I would gladly leave Denver. It was too big, I was out of my element.

I heard, providentially it seemed to me, that in Longmont, a small town some forty miles north, there was a butcher shop for sale. Though I didn't know much about butchering, I had learned a lot about cattle on the farm; if I could get a butcher shop, no doubt I could hire a meat cutter; if I bought the livestock the work would keep me out in the open. That way I would be following the doctor's orders.

I liked the look of Longmont, sent back to Mother for my savings, and arranged to buy the butcher shop. I hired a meat cutter and, rather proudly, I admit, had my name painted on the window in big letters, *J. C. Penney.* A bull's head was pictured above the name. Later I sometimes wondered if there had been something prophetic in that.

My meat cutter immediately offered some well-meant advice. "You want to look after the chef at the hotel," he said. Our backlog of trade came from the hotel.

"Look after him? What do you mean? How? Why?"

"You're supposed to give him a bottle of bourbon once a week. He's mad that you haven't done it yet."

"Why should he expect whisky from me?"

"For giving you the hotel's trade. He told me today if you don't start getting a bottle over to him, bing! no more orders."

Looking back on the episode from this year of 1960 it occurs to me that perhaps my situation with the chef was an early form of the now deplorable "payola" practice. At all events, from what the meat cutter told me, I could tell I was pretty green and had a lot to learn.

I bought the bourbon and took it to the chef. My first thought was that I mustn't lose my venture. My conscience troubled me, though. I didn't need to ask myself what my father would say if he knew I was bribing—the right word, ugly though it was—a man with whisky to favor me with his trade! Father would simply point out that what I was really doing was compromising principle. I worried my decision backward and forward in my mind. I hated to lose business, and the hotel order was profitable.

A phrenologist came to town to give a lecture and I went. The posters proclaimed that he could foretell one's future from the bumps on your skull. A large audience filled the hall and the man called for volunteers to come up on the platform so that he could demonstrate. I went up, with six or seven others.

He put quite a lot of showmanship into fingering our head-bumps. He asked each person what business they were in. I said I had a butcher shop. He took a step backward and, staring at me, exclaimed, "You don't really mean that, do you? Why, you'll never be a success with a butcher shop." He fingered the bumps some more, adding, "Now you'd be a good railroad builder, or a banker." In later years when I recalled the incident I noted that he never mentioned merchant. Some of my associates used to laugh, "Well, thank the Lord you failed as a butcher!"

I let the hotel chef know that I would not continue supplying the weekly bottle of whisky. He was as good as his word to the meat cutter, cutting off the hotel meat order. Soon I lost the butcher shop—in its way, I suppose, a kind of testimonial to the phrenologist's art! I sometimes wondered if he ever chanced to learn how right he had been about my not succeeding as a butcher. But then we live and learn. Probably I should never have undertaken a butcher shop in the first place. Around home there was a popular saying, "Well, I admire his grit, but durn his judgment!" I once heard it applied at a railroad switch point, when a car was cut out of a freight train and a bull calf broke through a fence and rushed at the car, trying mightily to butt it off the track. My father might have had a respect for my grit in trying to run a butcher shop but probably not much for my judgment.

I found employment with a Longmont merchant, in his store T. M. Callahan & Co. The store was not unlike that of the Hales, back in Hamilton and, for me, was thus a return to familiar ground.

When I applied for a job my amateurishness with the butcher shop had preceded me. Mr. Callahan said, with a slight, friendly smile, "Young man, we sell drygoods—we don't have much use for a butcher in our store." He was having a bit of fun with me, at the same time putting me at ease; being a man with heart, he saw that what had happened was a big disappointment to me.

I wanted very much to work in his store but of course I had no way of foreseeing that I would learn from him a way of doing business as a merchant which would become one foundation stone of my whole business life.

A clerk of his was sick, the holidays were drawing on, and I was hired as a substitute, with the pretty clear understanding, however, that it was only temporary.

This gives me an opportunity to suggest a thought with regard to "temporary" jobs. Many people have the experience at one time or another of being hired as temporary help. The "temporary" factor offers a choice of attitude. One can work just enough to "get by," the idea being that it won't much matter, since they won't be staying on anyhow. Or one can work as though, if one showed one's mettle, the job would either become permanent, or something as good or better would come of it. Naturally I am in favor of the latter attitude. No telling where it may lead, what it may open up in the way of opportunity.

When the regular clerk returned, Mr. Callahan called me aside, saying, "Young man, would you be interested in going over into Wyoming to help my partner, Guy Johnson, in his Evanston store?"

"If you haven't got anything for me here, yes, I'd like it fine." I wanted to stay in Mr. Callahan's store. I had found out I could learn a lot from him. More important, I saw that he would like to keep me on, which showed I had made myself useful to him.

"Well, Guy Johnson needs a man and I've told him you'll do well for him." He then explained to me the arrangement between himself and Mr. Johnson. It was a partnership plan along new lines; though still in its formative stage, they were developing it. Briefly, Mr. Johnson had first worked in the Longmont store for Mr. Callahan. Then, observing his capability and that he would work well on his own, Mr. Callahan located another store in Evanston, putting Johnson in there as manager and partner, Johnson's investment coming out of his savings from the Longmont job.

"We're going to work up a string of stores in different towns through Colorado and Wyoming," Mr. Callahan explained to me. "Make the most of your opportunity with Johnson, and you may get your own store some day, with Johnson and me as your partners."

In my surprise and enthusiasm I forgot to ask what my salary would be. When I got to Evanston I found out it would be $50.00 a month; enough, I decided, to warrant my asking a young lady I had met and begun keeping company with,

Miss Berta Hess, to marry me. Five months from the time I began working in Evanston, I went to Cheyenne. Being low on ready cash I borrowed a mileage book for the trip and we were married.

The next summer the Mayor of Evanston made me an offer to work in his store, salary $100 a month. The store was a good one, the money inviting, but there was an ethical problem. I had been well treated by Mr. Johnson and learned a great deal; I couldn't see how I could accept any offer without first talking it over with him.

"Well, I can't stop you, Jim," he said, "but I hope you don't take it. Callahan and I will be branching out—as we get new stores, we'll need good men to open and manage them. It's still ahead of us and I can't promise anything, but you've had time to see how it can work on a larger scale, and I don't believe you'll lose in the long run by staying here with me now." I agreed with him, and stayed.

Some time later the partners began planning to open a new store in Ogden. They said they wanted me to open it, and be their partner. It seemed out of the question from my standpoint. Why, they had $10,000 invested in shoes alone in the Evanston store! I did not have enough money to swing a third share in a partnership. I pulled back from the proposal, on the ground that I was just a farm boy, and Ogden was too big a place for me. Mr. Johnson laughed.

"You and Mr. Callahan are a lot more alike than you know; that's what he says, 'Ogden's too big.' I argue, however, that we want to do big things and, if we're going to succeed, we have to go for the cities." He enumerated some of Ogden's advantages; five banks, a public library, twelve churches, an opera house seating 2000, a brewery, many schools, three parks, telephones, electricity, and more than 35,000 people to be converted into customers.

"I'd rather go somewhere else, Mr. Johnson," I said. I imagined that I could hear Father's voice; "Now, Jim, don't go putting your mind against the older man's experience."

"Where, then?" said Mr. Johnson.

"Well—Diamondville."

"Ever been there?"

"No."

"Then why——"

"Diamondville people come to Evanston to trade—that means they don't find what they want in Diamondville. Besides, they're the sort of people I'm used to; big-city people'd be strangers to me—I'd be a stranger to them——" It all sounded sensible to me, but Johnson thought I was wrong. However, Callahan said, "Jim, Kemmerer's the place for you, Diamondville isn't."

"Kemmerer? Where's Kemmerer? What kind of place is it?" It was a mining town, between Diamondville and Frontier. Mr. Callahan recommended that I go and look it over. But a few hours later I told the partners I'd take their word for it. The fact was the trip would cost me $15, and if I were going into partnership I'd need every dollar. I had $500 savings but even that would hardly be enough.

Mr. Callahan happened to hear something from an Evanston merchant and it made him question the wisdom of Kemmerer for me, after all. "Three sons of mine opened and operated a business in Kemmerer," this man had said, "and they failed, couldn't make a go of it." Mr. Callahan told his partner, Johnson, "Jim Penney is no brighter than those three boys; if they couldn't do anything with it, I don't know——"

Contradictorily, the more I thought about Kemmerer, the more it seemed the place for me. When Mr. Callahan couldn't discourage me, he worried, and finally asked Mrs. Penney to prevail on me to go somewhere else. Her response resembled that of Ruth, in the Bible. "Where Jim wants to go, I'll go," she said, and Mr. Callahan gave up.

"Johnson and I will lend you the $1500 you'll need for your third share," said Mr. Callahan.

"What will the interest be?"

"The going rate—eight per cent."

Back in Hamilton there were two banks. I would write one first and, if necessary, the other. I got the money I needed.

"You went to all the bother of negotiating with a bank back in Hamilton?" said Mr. Johnson, puzzled. "Why?"

"I saved two per cent interest; got the money for six per cent, and all it cost me was a two-cent postage stamp."

As a town, Kemmerer was certainly barren and unprepossessing. Without shade trees or other softening touches of nature, spring was late that year of 1902, frost was coming out of the ground reluctantly and the streets, such as they were, ran with a mushy mud. Among mining employees, ranchers from the surrounding country and the mercantile people gravitating to any raw young community there were many nationalities, and I believe the first Orientals I ever saw were there in Kemmerer. An incident occurred later which particularly impressed the Chinese on me.

The explanation of their unique partnership, given me by Mr. Callahan and Mr. Johnson, registered in my mind clearly enough but for a considerable time I was so busy getting this store established that I thought very little about its leading to anything outside Kemmerer. We began before sun-up and

I never closed our doors until I saw with my own eyes that the streets were empty of possible customers. I soon learned that people were saying I was money-mad. I didn't think of it that way; a young man, with a wife and baby to provide for, starting out in business in a location previously dominated by company stores, had to look sharp if he expected to make a living. Mine was an honest business and there was certainly no call to apologize for wanting to make it pay as well as I could. I noticed that the saloon-keepers were not called money-mad, although of course they did not stay open quite as late, or open up as early as our Golden Rule store. And, along with needing to succeed, the trade the store attracted from the first day began to take hold of my imagination. Late at night, while I cast up the day's receipts, larger ideas stirred around in my mind. Why, there was no telling where this thing might take me! But I mustn't let my imagination run away with me. In earlier years my father sometimes discerned a habit in me of jumping to conclusions. He used to caution me and, as so often was the case, his admonitions took hold in my mind. "You want to curb that impulse to jump to conclusions, Jim," he would say; "if you don't look out, you'll never amount to anything." Sometimes it was thought that he was too critical, too severe; but I knew, everybody knew, that he had our best interests at heart.

Mr. Callahan came through on a trip and explained enthusiastically that he had it in mind now to piece together a chain of fifty stores. "Jim, I have the idea of putting you in charge of them," he said.

I had not felt ready to attempt Ogden, I certainly didn't feel ready for the responsibility of managing any fifty stores. I have never been an advocate of throwing a person into the water over his head in order to teach him to swim. Of course, sometimes it will work, but not always. In a long business life I have seen many men harmed by being given responsibility they were not ready for. As for myself, I wanted to get ahead, but by building carefully as I went. Along with selling merchandise—there were some differences between selling goods as a clerk, and selling them as a proprietor—I was building business policies on personal concepts of integrity. For example, on buying trips I made a point of testing merchandise to my own satisfaction before buying. How could I represent a value to my customers as the best for the money unless I knew for a fact, beyond all doubt, that it was the best?

I simply didn't know enough yet to be put in charge of fifty stores, and told Mr. Callahan so. He smiled, implying that it was only a matter of time.

I had grown up to admire neighborliness but must admit, in the days of getting established in Kemmerer, the length of my working day left little time and thought for anything but business. One night an incident occurred which rather abruptly presented me with the necessity of making time to respond to a call for help.

A few yards from my store there was a Chinese laundry. I had bought my first house, and we were living just across from the store.

One night, when we were sleeping the sleep of the bone-tired, I was waked up by a loud cry, as of someone seemingly in great pain, and a heavy rapping on our front door. My wife begged me not to answer, for she feared desperadoes of some kind. "Whoever it is will go away if you don't answer," she whispered.

"But that was the cry of someone in trouble," I whispered

back. "I have to see what I can do." I put on a bathrobe, and when I lit a lamp and opened the door, there stood the laundryman. Nobody in town was able to have much converse with him for his English was pretty much limited to the proverbial. "No check-ee, no shirt-ee," so to speak.

He was very agitated, speaking rapidly and unintelligibly but with many gestures. I couldn't make anything out of the torrent of words in his native tongue but gathered from the gestures that he wanted me to come with him at once. He kept pointing at the store across the road. It was almost one o'clock in the morning but he seemed to want me to come with him and open the store. There was no way for me to understand his reason but I didn't like to turn him away. I indicated to him somehow that, if he would wait a moment, I would get on some clothes and go with him.

We hurried across the road, I unlocked the door and lit the coal-oil lamp. In addition to the stock on counters and shelves a lot of our merchandise had to be hung on lines overhead.

The Chinese looked everywhere, obviously searching for something particular. Suddenly, jabbering excitedly, he pointed upward, pacing about nervously, waiting for me to get the article down. It was a woman's white muslin nightgown. He had no family and I was more mystified than ever.

I got down the garment. Trotting anxiously back and forth, nodding, chattering, gesticulating, it was evident that he wanted me not to wrap it. He kept beckoning insistently, and I fathomed that he wanted me to go across with him to his home.

We reached the tiny room at the back of his shop; in the murky light another Chinese, half sitting up, half lying on a bed in the corner, eyes wild and staring, was making primitive, hysterical sounds. What he was saying was undistinguishable but he was clearly in terrible distress, and I sensed that he was dying. The laundryman was talking rapidly now. He made urgent gestures in my direction and I somehow gathered that the garment procured from the store was to be put on the terrified man. Together we held the thrashing figure firmly enough to dress him in the white nightgown; although it was a woman's garment it didn't seem to matter. Once it was on, he seemed to ease a little. He subsided on the bed, moaning and whimpering. It seemed all right for me to go and I went home.

I learned the next day that the man had died before sun-up.

It was a very strange experience and I asked questions until I found someone who could explain it. It seems that it is traditional among the Chinese that one must not arrive in the presence of his ancestors without being dressed suitably in white.

We had not had any way to communicate with each other in words; as time went on that situation did not change, for the laundryman's English remained nil, and I never learned any Chinese. Yet I had learned how much people can want to be treated just as people. I, in turn, had been given the chance to do a service. Service was as much a part of the sign over my store as the merchandise inside.

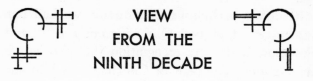

CHAPTER IV

Human Relations—Our Most Important Commodity

We are prone to interest in the careers of "self-made" men, so-called. Yet I cannot recall knowing of anyone who made success by himself. Whether we recognize it or not, we are inextricably bound with one another. John Donne put his finger on it a long time ago when he wrote, ". . . no man is an island . . ."

Experiences in business which remain forcibly with me are linked by this factor of interdependence. "Economic history," Gabriel Hauge pointed out "is the chronicle down through the ages of man's efforts to match limited resources to unlimited needs. . . ." *

Very early, in exploring the possibilities of Callahan and Johnson for a chain of stores linked by their partnership idea, I perceived that, unless I found men to help me, I could not

* Commencement Address, Bryant College, Providence, R.I., Aug. 1, 1958.

succeed, nor, unless I reciprocated their help, could those men succeed.

At the outset in Kemmerer, naturally we had our hands full, just to get established. Observing business life nowadays, I notice more and more recognition that the key factor is human relations. The plan of Callahan and Johnson to expand, perhaps to as many as fifty stores (though for some time I was more inclined to think of twenty-five as a goal), made it plain to me that the first and greatest asset would be *men*.

At first, in Kemmerer, my wife and I did most of the work. On slack days I could do it all myself, with Mrs. Penney coming down from the attic where we lived, to tend store while I ate my lunch or supper. On the miners' pay days I had extra help. In the fall of the first year I hired an extra clerk. There wasn't much book work to do, because I paid all the bills myself, and also "checked in" the merchandise. I had more help the second year, but still did most of the selling. My hardest job was the selling. It was a lot more than just showing articles and taking in money on sales. I had to satisfy the public that I could save them money. Most of the miners' wives did the shopping for the family, since the miners worked six days a week. I had to satisfy the miners' wives that I could sell them a pair of shoes for one dollar less than they could buy them in the company stores. Though Kemmerer was situated in the middle of a coal-mine district, actually there were no mines in the town. Before long, however, I was doing most of the miners' shoe business of the community.

In clerks, I looked for men who accepted hard work willingly, in fact welcomed it, coupled with enthusiasm for learning. A little later on I want to comment on the status of hard work today, and attitudes toward it.

At that time our clerks received about $75 a month. We worked seven days a week, opening up late on Sundays, at eight o'clock instead of seven, having worked extra late Saturday nights, and I got a reputation rather quickly for being a hard man to work for. Even if there weren't a customer in the store, there was plenty to be done; dusting and placing stock, and keeping the floor clean. The term "eye appeal" hadn't come into use then, but to me it was very important that a store should be inviting and, above all, immaculately clean. The store was small, we carried an abundance of merchandise, and at times there was the appearance of a jumble, but it was always a *clean* jumble. The clerks grew used to my proddings, "You have to keep busy; you're being paid for work, not for standing around, visiting, reading the paper—we're all business here." I now believe that I was a hard man to work for, although I never asked or expected any more of a clerk than I did of myself.

While what was to become the largest store chain of its kind in the world started from that idea of Callahan and Johnson, chains as such began long before them. Many centuries earlier a Chinese merchant devised a system for distributing goods through a large group of stores. In 1643 in Japan, the Mitsuis formed a chain of apothecaries which held leadership until the close of World War II. The China trade touched off the beginnings of the Great Atlantic & Pacific Tea Company, and other businesses came into being, operating on the chain plan "to bring to the consumer necessities at lower prices."

It remained for Callahan and Johnson to apply a unique variation to the chain system. I have always thought of it— not so much as a chain of stores as a chain of men and women, linked by an idea. By first training me, then putting me in charge of a store and making me their partner, and, finally, dissolving their partnership and selling out their interest in three stores to me, they put me in position, as you might say, to carry on the trust.

I did not spy on clerks to see if they were doing their job, I observed them. To me there is an important difference. The purpose of spying is usually to find something unworthy; of observing, to find something of good and constructive potential. When I devoted a spare moment to going over floor space with a broom where a clerk had swept before, I accomplished one or both of two things. I found any dust that had been missed; but, often, I found evidences of that thoroughness which marked the clerk for favorable attention. Having swept well, he showed himself interested in advancing.

A steady increase in sales made any clerk a potential candidate for a tryout manager and possible partnership later on. Certain factors ruled a man out altogether. We didn't have any place for cigarette-smokers, or those who used liquor either. Some people thought such rules of mine took in too much territory, but I was working toward a building operation and there was no sense in making a place for defective materials.

The Kemmerer store was going along quite well when an opportunity arose rather suddenly to test the asset or liability value of men. At about the same time Callahan, Johnson and I started our partnership in Kemmerer, they put a man in charge of a store in an adjacent community. He was not lacking in knowledge of operating a store but had an avocation which somewhat divided his interest. He wished to join the town band. There was a certain logic to it; he was a trombonist. Soon, however, when there were rehearsals to attend, or an extra five dollars to be earned by playing in a band concert, store sales showed marked signs of falling off. My partners thought I should become their partner in this store, too, and take the responsibility of its management.

Except for aggravated cause I am no believer in firing a man out of hand. That the first niche is not the right one does not necessarily mean that a man lacks potential. I wanted to give this man a chance to calibrate his position and opportunity. However, he turned out to be one of the exceptions to this reasoning, and was replaced. Sales were revived and I, too, had had an opportunity to learn from the experience.

I was taken by surprise when I learned one day from Callahan and Johnson that they had made up their minds to dissolve their partnership in their present stores. I had now been in Kemmerer five years, and they proposed that I buy out their interest in our stores, at this time numbering three.

On my forlorn trip to Denver in the stifling day coach, about the last thing I would have been able to visualize would be my signing a note for $30,000 at eight per cent. But they had fired me well with the possibilities of their idea, and I had come to a point where I could stand off and judge it at full circle because I had gone through its steps which were as follows: 1) manage a store; 2) train a man to be a manager; 3) open another store and place him as manager; 4) and, when he is able to finance his share out of his earnings, make him a partner.

I agreed to their proposition. All I could give them as a guarantee was my name on the note; they did not have to be convinced that to give them a lien against merchandise in the stores would be to impair my credit.

They took my signature. On a scale I would hardly have dared dream five years earlier, I was in business for myself. My capital was three stores and the operating ideal, "to find and train men capable of assuming responsibility, and a loyalty rooted in mutual confidence."

In later years it was to be said that I originated employee profit-sharing in this country. I could not accept that much credit, for several reasons. In the first place, from the early Kemmerer days, I thought of myself, not as an employer, but as an associate with men in a common enterprise, to the mutual interest and benefit of our customers and ourselves. We owed a service to our community. Unless our customers were able to save money on everything they bought, we had no right to be in business. We had to be constantly vigilant that, in pursuing ambition for success, we did not fall into the way of making too much profit, a lion's share. Lasting prosperity for ourselves would only come if the people of our communities were happier and better off for our being among them. Thus our relationship, in the framework of the partnership plan, was not that of employer-employee; it was a fellowship of associates in a common enterprise.

Not long ago I came across a dismaying statement made by a man who has achieved great success over a long period of time in the world of entertainment.

"A man can't live on principles," this man said. It shocked

me but it startled me, too, for it was so contrary to my practical experience. We started out by lining up our business dealings with the Golden Rule. I am often asked whether the Golden Rule, obviously "a nice ideal," hasn't become obsolete as an instrument for life in a practical world. I have to answer that, in the years since the beginnings in Kemmerer, I have never found any good reason to desert it. Moreover, traveling about over the country, it seems to me that I see more awareness and sincere effort to put into practice this ancient prescription for building fairness, service and brotherhood.

And why not? In one phrasing or another its principle is common to all great religions of the world; it is a stated tenet of at least eleven, including Buddhism, Christianity, Judaism, Taoism, Islam.

Rabbi Hillel, the great Jewish religious educator who lived shortly before Christ, expressed it in these words: "What is hateful to thee, do not do to another." Confucius, living in the sixth century B.C., said "Do not unto others that which you would not that they should do unto you." In the fourth century B.C. the noted Athenian orator Isocrates said, "What you are angry at, when inflicted on you by others, this do not to them."

Many look on the enunciation of the principle by Jesus Christ as the most perfectly expressed of all:

"Therefore, all things whatsoever ye would that men should do to you, do ye even so to them." This is a positive wording, which brings to mind a thought of Paul Tillich, since 1933 Professor of Philosophical Theology at Union Theological Seminary in New York. He comments that it was mostly in the negative form—"Do *not* do to others"—that the Golden Rule was known to Jews, Greeks, and others. And he emphasizes that the positive form is closer to love, though strictly it is not love, but rather calculating justice. By love, and only by love, can calculating justice be transformed into creative justice, for love establishes justice, making it just.

For more than ten years after starting out under it, at Kemmerer, I kept the name Golden Rule Store for doing business. It was more than a painted sign, it was the remembered voices and example of my parents, the principle they lived by and instilled.

We dropped it later, for external reasons. Its use had become casual in many places; to our way of thinking it had lost some of its meaning for the public. We did not have to proclaim the Rule to continue practicing the spirit. We let the name go but I believe firmly that, without having kept our hold on the principle in everyday practice, there would be no J. C. Penney Company today. We stayed in a long line of good company, reaching from times before Christ.

When I say that success has no secrets I am thinking of the Golden Rule as the pathway. There certainly are no secrets about the Golden Rule.

In line with the fellowship nature of seeking men with the capacities and vision to share in a common enterprise a view began to form in my thinking. Like a gem expert, turning and turning an uncut stone under the jeweller's loupe to consider its possibilities for refracting the light, I turned and turned it in my mind. The essence was that it will pay to be unselfish.

Now sometimes today, when I mention in a public talk

what became in time a very real part of my business philosophy, I can feel a catch of hesitancy in my hearers, until I show that it is not an attempt at a play on words, or a paradox.

I would never advocate unselfishness *for selfish reasons.* In business experience I have found that unselfishness pays *because it tends to engender unselfishness.* The life of our fellowship of association has always been a bond of common effort, unifying and stimulating the collective ambition. Results would not have been the same if the unselfishness—mutual interest, and benefit of our customers and ourselves—had been selfish, individual prosperity only. Since the principle was right, expansion was inevitable, and success both in terms of money and growth, could but follow.

Callahan and Johnson had, though not in so many words, given me my first insight into this. As time went on, one thing I was most to wish for was that, as we worked together, other men might, through me, experience the same energizing effects of faith and freedom of initiative which my partners had opened up to me by their confidence in sending me to Kemmerer.

I had as much to learn as did the men who worked with me. We didn't expect anyone to know it all and the thing we guarded against was acting as though we did. In addition to being good workers, we wanted men to be good-humored but we were understandably not interested in anything bordering on the smart-aleck. In that connection I recall a man I interviewed, who had applied to come with us. In the course of finding out about him, I asked if he drank liquor or smoked cigarettes.

"No," he said airily, "and I don't crochet either." I never felt quite sure whether he understood why he wasn't accepted.

Not wanting smokers had a sound, practical reason. In the early days space was usually cramped and we carried large stocks of merchandise. Smoking on the premises produced a fire hazard. But over the years I have known of many men who gave up smoking in their wish to make good in our business.

This is a good place to mention why I made it a practice to interview wives of men too. When a wife is in close sympathy with her husband's aspirations and the nature of his work, she can be a very real support to him. And I believe women are possessed of strong intuition which, when they are keenly interested in supporting a husband's ambitions, can materially help his advance.

Once, in a letter, I had to sum up reasons for letting a man go and I wrote, "He wasn't active, couldn't get a move on him; and he didn't know the first thing about dry goods." If he had had a wife, with a woman's natural endowment of intuition, things well might have been quite different.

It may seem, that to keep store in a small town, all that would be necessary would be to have adequate stock, open the door in the morning, wait on customers and count up the receipts at night. It was not quite that simple and I am glad that it was not. In the same way that I had had to work my mind hard, in my school years, to figure out how to make a nickel or a dime, in selling to miners, ranchers and their families the goods they came in needing to buy, we had to know a lot more than just price marks, and what shelf the men's cotton flannel drawers were on.

I kept a little penny notebook in my pocket. Gradually it became a thesaurus which I can still consult today. It was much more of a guide to business than a mere day-to-day list of goods sold for a stated amount of profit. For example, I know now what the weather was on a given day in 1905 because weather had a direct and important effect on sales. When late fall was unseasonably mild, we could be sure of slow sales of heavy underwear. If there were no snow, and cold weather held off capriciously, overshoes wouldn't move. However, even though the ground remained bare of snow, if the thermometer should drop well below zero in the night, we had to be ready for the people who would hustle in and buy overshoes, to keep their feet warm. We couldn't afford guesswork but had constantly to study, and wherever possible anticipate, our customers' needs, know our markets and watch our inventory. In our lexicon there was no place for the words, "Sorry, we don't have your size"; neither could we operate on the system of early mark-ups and later mark-downs. People sometimes remarked that we didn't seem to run many "special sales." Indeed we didn't. We didn't want the customer paying the bill for curing our mistakes.

Happily there were many items we could sell in any weather. For example, clothespins, two cents a dozen, and clothesline, eighteen cents per fifty feet.

In some ways our requirements of a man who would fit in with our opportunities ran parallel with those of any going business. In our particular case, we needed a man experienced in all lines of general dry goods; capable; not afraid of work; a man of integrity, not afraid of responsibility. But then there was that extra something—the wish and capability to adapt himself to and become part of our principles. In time it was to become recognizable as a distinguishing spirit of our company.

Our all-around aim reminds me now in some ways of a

thought expressed by Carl Schurz: "Ideals are like stars. You will not succeed in touching them with your hands. But, like the seafaring man in the desert of waters, you choose them as your guide and, following them, reach your destination."

The more I thought about the partnership idea and sharing in its growth—and, owing $30,000 at eight per cent, I thought about it concretely as well as abstractly—I saw how the opportunity it presented was a two-way street: an opportunity for me in offering it; equal opportunity for those to whom it was offered. It laid a big obligation on me to estimate men's powers well, not bring them in unless they were suited, not push them ahead before they were ready. My function would in certain respects be fiduciary.

One rule I set myself was that no man who came in would be under bond. I never think a halter around a man's neck will be what makes him want to do the right thing. Thus from the outset any man was left free to break away if he chose. It put the whole burden on character which, first and foremost, was what I was after in men.

None of us is born possessing character. Character finds its own form in the adjustments we make to conditions in which we find ourselves, in the attitudes and choices we bring to bear on problems presenting themselves to us to be solved.

The only bond worth anything is the moral bond. Men of character don't break moral bonds. If we picked men carefully, we would have no cause for worry, and would build a fellowship which would renew itself from within.

It is sometimes said that ethics and economics are separate and distinct from each other. I don't see it that way. A moral bond in the economic climate will impart strength far exceeding that of money.

By such steps and reflection, our pattern for the future approached definition.

Best in men, best in service, best in price.

The principle of our dealings being right, in the natural course of things the success in money would take care of itself.

I won't say that conducting our dealings by the Golden Rule principle was always, or consistently can be, easy. Nor would I say that, to be successful in business, it is only necessary to refrain from sharp practices. But I do say that it is possible to live and conduct business successfully on principle. It was because of the proofs I have both experienced and witnessed, that I was so startled by the statement earlier quoted. As I thought it over, I hoped the man had been misquoted.

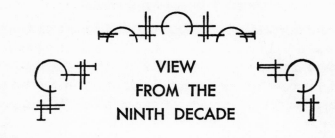

CHAPTER V

Christian Principles Win in Business

A woman wrote me from her small store in a mid-western town, saying, "Come to see me, and tell me some of your tricks." I gathered she had two thoughts in mind, in seeking this merchant-to-merchant exchange. She mentioned that she was eighty years old, so evidently she saw no good reason why a vigorous woman should stop working just because she was up in years. Her wanting to hear about some of our "tricks" must be because she inferred that it would be difficult for one small mining-region store to grow into a chain of almost 1700 stores, located in forty-eight out of the fifty states, without shrewd practice along the line. We did build shrewdly on thrift, common sense and fair dealing, but I wouldn't regard those as tricks.

It would of course be evasive to imply that, like Topsy, we "just growed." The seven years I stayed in Kemmerer were very hard years indeed. It is sometimes easier to turn a hundred dollar profit today than it was to turn a nickel profit then. Prospects for expansion did appear, but we had to learn to stand up before we could walk, and to walk before we could run. However, we formulated business methods which could be adapted to an expanding operation. Their main and most far-reaching characteristic was our code of *Christian Principles in Business*. Experience has shown their power to be positive. Their common denominator is that *they win*. I would like to share them in capsuled form with the reader.

Preparation wins. Demonstrably, accomplishment is linked closely to preparation. Admitting that I am myself more typical of what nowadays is classified as "on-the-job training," a person must start out by knowing all he can about his job, and never stop learning as he goes along. I can cite an illustration in my own preparation.

In the early years my partners Callahan and Johnson took me to market in New York. One night I took samples of the wholesaler's piece goods back to my hotel room. I washed them and pinned them up to dry on the Nottingham lace curtains. Would the cloth shrink? Was it fast color? I needed to know all I could find out, about how it would act when customers used it.

Mr. Callahan stopped in to speak to me about something. When his eye fell on my "wash, hung out to dry," he burst out, laughing wryly, "What's all this for?"

"Before buying, I'm making sure the goods are as represented."

"But the wholesaler told you——"

"Yes. But it'll be my word that the customers go on. I must be sure."

Mr. Callahan shook his head. "You'll never get to be a big merchant, spending time this way."

"Maybe not," I replied. "I think I'd better get to be a good one, though, before I try to be a big one."

Hard work wins. It is often said of businessmen and others who achieve a measure of success, "Oh, he was lucky. He started at the right place at the right time." It has been said of me.

I never believed in "luck." Growth and success don't come by chance. Determination, sacrifice of non-essentials, perseverance and hard work are all the luck needed.

We seem to be in an era of seeking to get everything we want with as little effort as possible on our part. Among many job applicants there seems to be a tendency to look more for security than for opportunity. Sometimes they will question a prospective employer before giving him a chance to question them! Do you have a pension plan, they want to know. Will I get paid vacations? Do you give regular raises? Do you have group insurance? How soon can I make $10,000 a year?

Recently I observed the contrasting approaches of two men as to a prospect which promised hard work with great opportunity.

Said one of them briskly, "When will I be getting my store?" His eye was on a managership.

The other man said, "This company is growing. What can I do to prepare myself for growing with it?"

Don't misunderstand me. I don't undervalue the importance

and power of security. I simply believe it comes through one's own hard work rather than externally or by chance.

When we were beginning to build a body of men, we didn't do much talking about security. But we talked a great deal about opportunity. The kind of men we were looking for could recognize that if they put opportunity first, the security would come in due course. People not afraid of hard work always stand out among those who see hard work as something to be avoided if possible.

I realize that tremendous sociological and economic changes have come to the country in the last thirty years. Many of them were overdue and are good. Heavy emphasis on security is closely tied in with changing attitudes as to just protection of individual rights including health benefits, retirement rights, and so on.

Speaking just for myself, I can't see why anyone would want to "retire." I never saw a fish that did well for long, resting on a bank, no matter how pleasant the grass, how warm the sun.

Personally I deplore that a man must work less, on pain of losing his social security safeguard. I see a great many people, compelled by statute to "retire" who neither physically need nor in their hearts want, to do so. For example, recently after returning from an extended trip, I went to my regular barber for a haircut. Instead of finding him at his chair, I was told that he was now working only Thursdays and Fridays; if he wanted his social security to remain undisturbed he was, by law, only "allowed" to work two days a week. Having observed him through a number of years, I doubt if enforced vegetation appeals to him; in fact, I wouldn't wonder if it takes more out of him than work ever did. However, once laws are on the books, of course, it is very hard to get them off. And, as I have said, changing conditions have produced some measures which, both economically and philosophically were needed, and are good.

Attitudes vary as to the value of hard work, certainly. It has been said "people seldom recognize opportunity because it comes disguised as hard work." This is undoubtedly somewhat oversimplified but, being particularly interested in young people's self-development, I can assure them that hard work brings many plus values, and that putting that *something extra* into work finds a special kind of reward. My friend the Rev. Ralph Sockman, recently observed in a sermon that people he saw playing solitaire never looked as though they were having a good time. For my part I have noticed that *clock-watchers never seem to be having a very good time.* And that people, conspiring all the time with themselves to get out of work as quickly as possible, always appear to be missing something. On the other hand, I have observed people who, although doing work which intrinsically was thoroughly routine, nevertheless managed to make it *personally creative;* by putting something extra into it, something of themselves, they discovered an extra value, a value of work for its own sake.

Honesty wins. When we speak in the abstract of honesty there is, of course, no difference of opinion. Nor am I thinking only of honesty as that quality which keeps a man from being light-fingered, taking something which belongs to someone else.

There are actually several kinds of honesty. One which

interests me particularly is that finer honesty, which prevents a man from giving less than his best—which bids him count, not his hours of work, but the opportunities his work affords him.

I believe much tension and dissatisfaction in the world of business arises out of too many people's trying to get material gain without giving their best. For example, the clerk who fools his customer, palming off on him some service or article of second-rate value, is first of all fooling himself. Second-rate standards never make a first-rate person. The individual who doesn't give what the finer honesty demands—his best—may and, in a measure, sometimes does, succeed; but the success not only falls short of what might be but will be of a kind which collapses under pressure.

When our business was started in 1902 I was unalterably convinced that practice of Christian principles was essential for success. I have certainly seen success come to men who ignored Christian principles altogether. If anything, it only strengthens my conviction that, now more than ever, the very complexity of our cultural and economic pattern, with its dominating human factors, makes their practice vitally necessary.

Confidence in men wins. My most valuable associates have been discovered through giving men responsibility and letting them know I relied on them. We hear a good deal, pro and con, on ways "to get good men." I believe the business community can make more use of the creative values of believing in men, stimulating their initiative by giving them responsibility, trusting in them.

The spirit wins. I have never been very interested in getting men just because they could carry out orders.

The Scriptures tell us, "For the letter killeth, but the spirit giveth life."

Fifty years ago and more a man could, so to speak, put religion in one compartment of his life, his business relations in another, and achieve a measure of success. The assumption was that business is secular, and service is religious. I have never been able to accept that line of arbitrary demarcation, and it seems less valid to me today than ever.

Is not service part and parcel of business? It seems to me so; business is therefore as much religious as it is secular. If we follow the admonition to love God, and our neighbors as ourselves, it will lead us to understand that, first of all, success is a matter of the spirit.

When I observe a young man or woman paying such close attention to service through their work that the closing hour can pass unnoticed, I know I am seeing the beginnings of success. Such people are showing themselves willing to give more than is required of them; *first* they are giving according to their spirit.

Practical application of the Golden Rule wins. It ensures obedience to civil law, but carries on past that letter of the law to the spirit which giveth life. It imbues us with the willingness to sacrifice personal interest if necessary for the good of others; in some cases even to deny ourselves indulgences which, though seemingly harmless to us, might work harm in the lives of others.

Most normal human beings have the instinct and disposition to defend the weak against the strong. Generally speaking, the spirit of the Golden Rule is present in our ideals of public and private well-being. We need to go farther in translating the spirit into concrete reality.

No family, society or other association of men can function effectively unless codes of conduct are set up. From the beginning of recorded time these have been expressed in varying forms. Basically all have agreed that man is endowed with certain rights but they are possessed within his relations to his Maker, and his neighbors.

Often we speak of the responsibility of us all, as Americans, to reflect and express America to the world. We can do so without chauvinism because, with the beginnings of our country, the Scriptures, and spiritual and moral values, were placed first.

William Penn well said, "He who will not be governed by God will be governed by tyrants." It seems to me this can be interpreted to mean that those who will not govern their dealings in life situations by Christian principles will find themselves being governed by "tyrants" such as dishonesty, greed and unjust conduct.

In the beginnings of what became our company, we chose Christian principles for the unifying thread. They furnished us a window on an unlimited horizon by putting the spirit first.

CHAPTER VI

Man's Natural Expression Is Work

Experiences come to people on which they can look back ultimately and say, "Here I recaptured the will to go on."

It has been said that experience is not what happens to us, it is what we do with what happens to us. At Christmas time, on the eve of leaving for the honeymoon trip we had not been able to take at the time of our marriage, Berta, my wife, died suddenly, inexplicably it seemed, for the immediate cause was trivial.

I was so overwhelmed by tragedy that, for some time, I did very badly indeed with what had happened to me. The assurance that God works in mysterious ways echoed through my mind as the worst sort of mockery; I felt hopelessly deserted by Him. I wandered about, helplessly envying those able to meet such experiences with fortitude and faith. I felt almost fatally drawn to drinking for escape, though I had never touched liquor in my life. I entertained the terrible knowledge that suicide could take me out of it all, when I couldn't stand it any longer.

I had grown up in acquaintance with prayer. Often, as my mother went about her housework, I heard her murmur a prayer, "Lord, be merciful to me, a sinner." It never failed to move me, for the rather unusual reason that I couldn't conceive of anyone being less a sinner.

But now, when I so desperately needed a power beyond my own, to save my reason and perhaps my very life, I realized I did not know how to pray.

On my first trip to New York in the early part of the new year, in my endless wanderings of the city I drifted down along the Bowery. Perhaps I thought that the sight there of sorrows worse even than my own would in some way shock me back to myself.

One night a fragment of familiar music caught at me from the open door of a mission for derelicts. It was a hymn we used to sing back home in Hamilton; "Jesus, lover of my soul." I went inside and slipped into a rear seat. I heard men telling how far they had run before meeting God, who touched them and led them back from despair. I told myself that I must have been led to this place, that there must be something here for me to know, to take hold of—but what?

Back in Salt Lake City, when it had become time for our boys—we had two then—to go to Sunday School, we had commenced attending a Methodist church. In my trouble its pastor, the Rev. Francis B. Short, had been devotedly standing by me. Now finally, with his two boys and mine, and a retired merchant, Newell Beaman, whom I had known in Evanston when I was with Guy Johnson, I went to Europe and the Holy Land. Perhaps in some vague way I thought that, among historical reminders of the ancient spiritual truths, I would find the anwer, be supplied a reason and the will to go on.

The elementary truth came to me that one can never escape himself. One may run far and long, resorting to all sorts of ingenious devices for escape, but in the end one will be able to face problems only when one is able to face oneself.

I have read somewhere a piece of advice out of the experience of a famous novelist, counseling young writers. "Don't look for the weaknesses in your work," he said, "look for the strengths." Very wise advice.

We sailed for home. I knew I had stopped running. I began to look for the strengths, not the weaknesses, of my situation. Were not my true capacities unimpaired, my opportunities undiminished, my business principles as workable as they had been, long before I made them mine.

Operating now under our profit-sharing partnership system, there were about thirty-five stores. That was a strength in itself, an inspiration; not a great while earlier I had felt I could be well satisfied with having an interest in twenty-five stores. All right for me, perhaps, if that were as high as I wanted to set my sights. But what about the men who joined their aspirations with mine, who wanted to go as far as *their* capacities would take *them*? Besides the opportunities for myself, there were my responsibilities to opportunities for these others. The heart of the partnership plan is the *liberation of men to work independently*. Men work best when they work for themselves. That is not to discount team work; the best team work I know of is men who are working independently toward one goal in unison. I began asking myself with interest, "Where are we going from here?" a question

I had scarcely had the heart in a long time to pose to myself.

A line in *The Tempest* seemed to answer me: "What's past is prologue."

Although it is taken out of chronology, this reminds me of an incident involving that statement and a rather succinct definition of its meaning.

A friend was riding in a taxi in Washington, and happened to notice Shakespeare's line carved over the lintel of the National Archives building.

"What's the meaning of that?" the fare said to the taxi driver.

" 'What's past is prologue'?" he said, disdaining traffic to look around. "Mister, it means you ain't seen nothin' yet!"

I disembarked from the ship feeling that, though we had advanced in the ten years since our beginnings, actually we hadn't seen anything yet. I felt reborn. I had a sense of electric anticipation, of standing on the threshold of greater opportunity than I had ever encountered. I felt a fresh selectivity, as to things that mattered and as to non-essentials. Although we had developed markedly, I think I might compare the enlarged perspective on resuming work to the resolve of a man to go from small studies in water color to murals of large dimensions and complex subject matter. To put it another way, the main purpose—giving men opportunity to share in and grow with what they themselves helped to create—was scaled up.

Although much emphasis is put on retirement and leisure time, man's natural expression and joy are in creative work. In my own mind I do not think of the term *creative* as limited in application to such arts as painting, music, literature. Whatever work a man does, if he puts something of himself into it, is creative. In this connection I might quote a bit of penetrating wisdom on the part of a New York taxi driver, bearing on the subject of doing a job well. I like the subway and don't ride much in taxis. When I do, however, I seldom fail to find some new evidence that the drivers are a rather exceptional group. It happened that this particular driver was colored; he was a tall, thin, reserved, soft-spoken man who was, he mentioned, over seventy years of age. I asked if he found driving in New York traffic conditions wearing. "The way I look at it," he replied quietly, "if you can't be proud of the way you do your work, what is there for you to be proud of?"

In the strictly business sense, we were at a critical stage. There were important internal and external adjustments and decisions to be made.

One of my first thoughts was that the name of the stores should be changed, and a corporate structure set up which would facilitate expansion, at the same time safeguarding the interests of each partner. Too, a centralized buying, accounting and credit system seemed indispensable to growth. Though a warehousing and bookkeeping system I had established in Salt Lake about four years earlier had fallen short of expectations, I was convinced of its essential value and prepared to revive the plan.

A number of our senior partners now were based in Salt Lake. I believed the logical location for the centralized operations was New York; the market being there, we would be efficiently close to our sources of supply. A much enlarged operation would require not only more men trained to be managers but also merchandise men, capable of wholesale buying, who were experts in credit and many other particulars.

The new plans were both ambitious and revolutionary. They had characteristics not to be found elsewhere in store operations. And yet, though I could demonstrate weaknesses in our existing operation, and opportunities for improvement, I met with resistance.

A banker, interested in my partnership philosophy, suggested that, since we had incorporated (primarily to comply with banking requirements to get money for expansion, inasmuch as I owned a majority of stock), I should simply compel my partners to go along with me on a move I was satisfied was sound. My friend was surprised when I explained that I could not compel them, for that very reason—because they were my partners. "We don't work individually," I said, "we work in unison."

Finally the partners did agree that, on my next buying trip to New York, Mr. Sams should go with me; when he returned to Salt Lake with a report on how the new plans would work in actual practise, they would listen to his conclusions.

Earl Sams had come with us in 1907. Like myself, he was a farmer's son, with a preference for storekeeping. One thing in his preliminary letters which impressed me was his insistence on knowing whether the job had *possibilities*. That convinced me that he was energetic and ambitious, not looking for a rut to slip into. I didn't paint him a picture of rosy conditions and quick success. Unless a man and his wife were all business, to my mind they'd better look elsewhere. This job was for a man who'd jump right in and keep at it all the time. The important thing was that such a man would find all the opportunity he could handle. Integrity, responsibility, initiative, ceaseless energy—we were looking for men who were men—and we knew they didn't come by, every day in the week. "You can have all the rope you want, Mr. Sams," I told him; "all you have to show us is that you know what to do with it." That he knew what to do with it is attested by the fact that, when I wanted to be relieved of the duties of president of the company, to concentrate on policies, and particularly on finding and training men to be our future executives, I placed his name in nomination, and one by one his partners, and mine, made his selection as president unanimous.

And so, fifteen years from the time of the Kemmerer beginnings, our sights could be raised again.

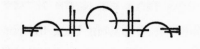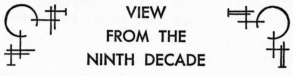

CHAPTER VII

The Learning Attitude Is Important

Here and there in this collection of thoughts I have linked literary allusions to certain points I wished to make. The reader may wonder how these allusions could come naturally to a man who only finished high school and even that, I am sorry to recall, with no great showing.

The explanation touches on a point which interests me greatly, namely, the permeating effect of the learning attitude. I recommend this point to the thought of anyone—from eight to eighty, as it were—who feels both the need and also senses the creatively useful pleasure of a more educated mind.

Go back to school! I did, and can hardly calculate what it has been worth to me ever since, in a variety of ways.

Once out of school, of course, there are many ways of a return to learning, whether in courses subsidiary to many types of employment, or for specialized extension courses, with or without scholastic credits, or purely as an avocation.

I was past forty when I went back to school. It grew out of recognizing that a businessman of rising success is called on by the press for interviews, and to give talks before various trade, civic and other groups. I felt a distinct deficiency about speaking acceptably in public and writing clearly; and I wanted generally to feel more at home in the world of ideas and literature.

For half of each business day through eighteen months, in an office I took in Aeolian Hall which was quiet and where I could concentrate without interruptions, I was tutored by Dr. Thomas Tapper whom I had come to know as a music critic and lecturer.

It broke a fixed habit of long standing—store visits—and in that period I hardly went out on the road at all. Dr. Tapper's method was to give me assignments, for both reading and written reports; we then discussed my grasp and interpretations of assigned subject matter.

I had certain long-range ideas in connection with it all, but wanted first to put myself under the discipline and influence of such work.

I made slow work of it at first. Dr. Tapper encouraged and reassured me by suggesting that men who are temperamentally active seldom are naturally word-minded; they incline to *doing* rather than to reading and talking. He cited many examples of men whose articulateness was limited though they carried large responsibilities outstandingly. I recall his speaking particularly of the Reverend Phillips Brooks, the great Boston cleric. He could talk well, so long as his subject was in the realm of the spiritual.

By this time our company had its New York headquarters on Seventh Avenue. In April of 1917 we inaugurated a company house organ, *The Dynamo*. Its basic purpose was to place in the hands of all our associates a working kit of facts, ideas and suggestions they might find stimulating and useful. As I worked along with Dr. Tapper I began to see the desirability of a well-arranged reading-and-study plan of which, though not compulsory in any way, Penney associates could avail themselves in line with their own aspirations for growth.

Dr. Tapper accompanied me on many store trips when the eighteen months of my concentrated study were up. He observed the range of characteristic methods in terms of manager to the newest salesperson. I finally asked him to exchange his work as critic and lecturer for educational work inside our organization. He was quite hesitant; it seemed to him problematical that a mercantile organization would be able to blend with its usual activities an educational plan of high quality.

This gives me another opportunity to stress the importance I place on the wives of businessmen. After Dr. Tapper decided to come with us he told me that it was Mrs. Tapper who convinced him that he should. Intuitively she had seen what could be accomplished in the way of real service, through our plans.

The resulting educational materials, as you would infer, placed great emphasis on the wisdom and value of preparation and on the folly of resorting to expedients, of compromise, of going into something you know nothing about. Theodore Roosevelt had an axiom that he liked to offer to young people. "Over, and never around!" he would cry, and his hearers could not miss the point which was the value of meeting any problem or job head-on.

I have spoken of our Salt Lake City pastor, Dr. Short. So

strong did my feeling grow that a team composed of Dr. Tapper and Dr. Short would be a tremendous impetus in what we were trying to do—develop leaders and trainers of men, and create new incentives and opportunities for promotion—that I proposed to Dr. Short that he join us. By now he had gone from Salt Lake City to a church in Spokane, Washington, where I often visited in his house.

As I had anticipated the talents of both men complemented each other, and tremendous good resulted. Both men traveled constantly to our store towns, speaking not only to our associates in the stores but to outside groups interested in hearing how we made watchwords of principles and, in terms of individual initiative, applied the Golden Rule concept to the broad task of doing business.

One great thing about the learning attitude is that it need never stop. I am always on the lookout for signs of it. I am elated when I observe people cultivating it, sorry when I see people neglecting it—sorry for the opportunity they are missing—and hopeful about even the "square peg" people because they may yet wake up. I have seen some very unlikely people who succeeded. Though their abilities were mediocre to begin with, they had that wonderful quality of not knowing when to quit. That, in itself, is evidence of the learning attitude.

I recall seeing a small printed sign once in a mechanic's place of business. "We do the possible right away," it read, "the impossible takes a little longer."

In the store of a merchant friend I stood one day, observing a young man who had not yet discovered the satisfactions to be had in a job well done. I asked my friend the proprietor how the boy was shaping up, for I knew something of his folks and his background.

"Jim," the merchant said, shaking his head regretfully, "I don't believe he's going to make it."

Just then a customer stepped up to the young man and asked to be shown unbleached muslin. He got the bolt down from the shelf and thumped it on the counter. I waited for him to talk it up to her; it was Double L muslin, an outstanding value among grades of unbleached muslin. But he only stood there, waiting for her to make up her mind. Either he didn't know about its quality or he was just too indifferent to talk it up. She bought the yardage and I wondered if he realized that it was in spite of him, not because of him. I could see why his employer did not believe the young man would make it; thus far, at any rate, the learning attitude made little appeal to him. It was not my place to volunteer my advice to him but how I wanted to! "Talk! Give! Assist!" I wanted to say to him. "Don't stop at yes or no. Radiate! Give of your time and yourself, even if you think you may not make the sale. You'll have held out both hands filled with service and the opportunity just to do that is one reward."

By contrast with my listless young friend, I remember an incident which happened to me in a railroad station lunchroom. In its way it was amusing, but it impressed me more because it was affirmative evidence for the learning attitude,

I had plenty of time for breakfast and ordered grapefruit, whole wheat toast dry, two medium boiled eggs, and Postum. "And I'd like the lower half of the grapefruit, please," I said to the waitress. She was typical of waitresses I had seen in station lunchrooms throughout my years on the road. A big-boned, fresh-skinned farm girl with a pleasant eye and a no-

nonsense air about her. I noticed that she shot me a curious glance, but she said nothing and went out to the kitchen to place the order. In a moment she was back.

"Mister," she said, "you did ask for the lower half of the grapefruit, didn't you? The chef says I'm crazy or deaf, one or the other. I'm beginning to wonder, myself. I been a railroad lunchroom waitress fifteen years and I never heard anyone wanting the bottom half of a grapefruit before."

I smiled.

"You're neither deaf nor crazy—that's what I asked for, all right."

"Mind me asking what's the idea?"

"Not at all. The bottom half has the most juice, that's all."

She laughed heartily.

"Well, Mister, thank you. Now I've learned something."

That was what left an impression in my mind, that after fifteen years on the job she knew she could still learn, and she enjoyed learning.

The wish to improve one's capacities and render better service invariably makes an impression on me, wherever I encounter it. Ambition and aspiration are innate in the American make-up. Examples of this are to be seen everywhere, and it goes without saying that willingness to learn has a great deal to do with them. I have always enjoyed recalling a young man who was a messenger for us in the early years, in our New York headquarters. He worked very hard all day but he had horizons he wanted to follow, so he went to night classes at Pace School. In time he became a tax expert and rose eventually to become company comptroller, with the responsibility for handling millions and millions of dollars.

I get the impression from some young people that their

attitude toward schooling and education is one of "what can't be cured must be endured." I don't believe they realize that they're not so much getting out of study as missing opportunities. I don't regret for a moment having, in effect, gone "back to school" at about the age of forty-two, tutoring for half of every business day for eighteen months. I wish I had made more of my opportunities in the years through high school, for their own sake at the time, and because I might have derived even more than I did—though it was a very great deal —out of the supplementary schooling.

I recommend this "hindsight" to young people for consideration.

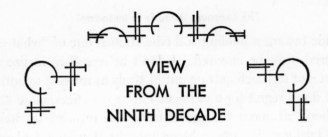

CHAPTER VIII

Success Cannot But Follow

The reader will have become aware that I am wholeheartedly committed to believing that, wherever human activity is conducted according to Christian principles of integrity, patience, unselfishness, humility, charity, diligence and fair-dealing, success cannot but follow. If it is possible to lead a Christian life at any point, it should be possible to lead it in all the relations of our lives. With God's help, the choice is ours.

Paderewski, Polish patriot and concert pianist, used to say ". . . take it where you will, creative work is the only thing in life that gives supreme satisfaction." To my mind, nothing is more creative than application of Christian principles to human endeavor.

Although it came about incidentally, stemming from a personal, unambitious cause, my embarking on what ultimately grew into an application of our company profit-sharing partnership plan to a project of improving the form and function of purebred cattle became, inevitably, creative in the best sense. To some it might seem that a merchant would be making a rather tangential move, from drygoods merchant to stockbreeder and farmer. In my case, on the contrary, it was but a step. Our normal merchant practices were simply adapted in different surroundings because the same principles could be applied to develop the farms as the stores. Nor, even though I had rejected it as a life work, was there anything odd in my turning interest to livestock and agriculture, for I had an inheritance of it through my grandfather and great-grandfather as well as my father.

My business had heavily impressed on my mind the bond between stores and rural people. We could have prosperity only if the farmer had prosperity; our well-being fell off in proportion to any falling-off of rural well-being. Thus our problems were bound together—theirs of buying goods they needed and wanted, at prices they could afford to pay; ours, continuing to serve them with values at fair prices.

Constantly traveling far and wide, I had a unique lookout post on agriculture in all its phases and effects. I became aware that in most sections the grade of beef and dairy animals was low. The greatest need of the farmer was better cattle. I asked many questions and received hard answers. For example, only three per cent of the cattle were purebreds; the average of butter-fat production for the country was 150 pounds per cow; that sort of thing. It should be remembered that I am speaking now of years on the eve of the Twenties. The picture would be somewhat changed for the better in the next twenty-five years—and still leave room for much improvement.

It happened at the time these harmful conditions were

being borne in on me, that I was feeling effects of what amounted to obsessive immersion in our business. The problems of growth were multiplying while the adventure and importance of what we were trying to accomplish were infinitely provocative to me. I was running health risks. I had warning. Just before leaving on a long and arduous itinerary, finding difficulty in sleeping restfully, I asked my doctor to give me a nerve tonic. "I'll give you no tonic," he said sternly, "but I'll give you some advice. If you don't cut down on the pace you're going, you'll be under the sod in five years." It was a shock to me also, on applying for $100,000 of life insurance, to be rated up ten years by two companies, thus halving the insurance I wanted.

In the interest of giving myself an incentive to more outdoor exercise, I acquired a small estate in Westchester County, and stocked it with a modest number of horses, cattle, sheep, poultry and a drove of Berkshire hogs. The Berkshires may have represented for me some nostalgic tie with my boyhood home. A poignant incident had revolved around a grievous disappointment, when my father's strict sense of fair dealing had forced me to get rid of a few pigs I had purchased after the most rigid saving, but which the neighbors complained about before I could get back my investment. I doubt if I was actually any more concerned now with the Berkshires than the rest of the animals, but at one point it became a standing joke with a minister-friend, visiting us for a week-end, that, while he spent an hour hunting high and low for me, I was with a farrowing sow, hovering over her with a large palmleaf fan because the thermometer had gone to 84 degrees and, poor thing, she was having a hard time of it.

In studying up on purebred cattle I came across the disturbing fact that every great herd built up in the United States had, upon the death of its owner, been dispersed to settle his estate.

I discovered that the average life of a breeding unit in America had been less than ten years, compared with an average of several hundred years in Scotland and parts of England. Furthermore, of herds in the United States that had been in existence for even as long as twenty-five years, there were few.

By degrees my mind turned to two rather large objectives which, though this was not their chief value, would afford a means of refreshing health and nerves through outdoor activity, and be possible to develop in accordance with the same principles underlying growth of the company.

I would set in motion a program to improve the form and function of purebred cattle; and I would do it on the unique basis of endowing herds, since the expected span of my life in any case would be all too short to work out all the possibilities I envisioned.

One of the first lessons I learned, as I got into the project, was the paramount importance of patience. Men who work in this field must be incorrigibly persistent, possessed by an indomitable, dogged patience. I well remember something written in the *Holstein-Fresian World* by Owen D. Young in 1940:

"Let no impatient man, who expects final results in a generation of cows, embark on the program," he said. "It takes a generation of men."

In reality, as I found out from experience, even that length of time is insufficient. Not infrequently a man engaged in this work must, as I once had to, face up to the fact that he has made a mistake and, summoning all his self-control and endurance, begin over again. Even when he meets with some success, he still must recognize that he falls short of perfection, and gird for further, doubtless even more strenuous, effort. Although he knows full well at this stage of the process that he may never succeed fully, his encouragement and spur alike will lie in the fact that he can make at least some tangible contribution toward that end.

I would recommend, to anyone tempted as I was by the real opportunities to turn a personal interest into a benefit to mankind, to school himself to recognize that the obstacles, like the encouragements, are many. The most important encouragement, perhaps, is that a solid foundation of accomplishment already exists. For example, high grade cattle of three breeds I mention here are available to whoever would enter the field. One has but to choose the breed with which he would like to work, and then follow the normal procedures, which are well-known. There is ample information available to guide anyone in beginning intelligently; the trail leading on toward perfection has been well charted, and a considerable body of knowledge already accumulated which is open to anyone.

The inspiring thought, that whatever progress the breeder makes benefits mankind, lifts him above the level of mere hobbyist, and certainly away from the selfish implication of sordid greed, endowing him instead with certain qualities of the philanthropist. It is a matter from which a man may take justifiable pride, to know that he has produced a better cow, horse, sheep or other creature, and to know that in such terms he has made as substantial a contribution to human welfare as though he endowed a hospital or built a library or school.

There is no doubt in my mind that the true breeder of purebred livestock possesses definite characteristics equipping him for that work. Primarily he is a scientist, since his work takes in principles of agriculture, horticulture, biology and animal husbandry, all demanding research, experimentation, study and sustained investigation. Fertility of the soil and its effects upon crops for feeding animals; relation of various foods to breeding, reproduction, diseases and their treatment —all these are important matters with which he must deal every day. Actually, no life calling touches a greater number of scientific tributaries than the breeding of purebred livestock.

And so, as I began to develop this interest as a business, history began repeating itself in the sense that, as in developing the company I personally selected each store manager, (until the time when the number became too great) I now proceeded on the line that *good men* would be as essential to success as good strains of cattle, and selected men who would fit in with the all-round concept for this project in livestock and agriculture.

In 1922 I acquired Emmadine Farm, a mile outside Hopewell Junction in Dutchess County, New York. After careful study I selected Guernseys, starting with the best Guernsey brood cows I could find, and four herd sires, among them Langwater Foremost, and joining the names Foremost Guernsey Association and Emmadine Farm. At the time of his purchase by me, Foremost was a sire of outstanding type and productiveness.

Emmadine had been the property of Robert Stuart. It was equipped at large expense of both money and time as a modern dairy plant with several hundred cows. While fully aware of the importance of dairy farms, and the production of clean, wholesome milk, I decided to make Emmadine a breeding rather than a dairy establishment. The soil had a fine limestone foundation, conducing to the good bone needed in breeding great cattle.

Foremost 39191 A.R. had sold in 1916 for $3000. Next he went to three Virginia dirt farmers for $5000, and finally to me for $20,000, a price which seemed to me moderate for a sire of the qualities judged by Gordon Hall, whom I regard as one of the greatest judges of cattle in the country.

In agriculture and the purebred cattle business, just as in the drygoods business, I proceeded on the philosophy that *honoring ideals of hard work and Golden Rule dealing with others* established a favorable climate in which to labor for the general good.

Foremost Guernsey Association, then known also as Emmadine Farm, was set up as a corporation to run until 1996, its property then to be transferred to the University of Missouri at Columbia for the use of its Department of Agriculture. It gave me deep personal satisfaction to ensure that, should I pass on tomorrow, my work would continue uninterrupted.

Soon the reputation of Emmadine Farm was not limited to this side of the Atlantic. The Isle of Guernsey is the ancestral home of Guernsey cattle, and the evolution of our Foremost Guernsey herd was watched over there with intense interest. As a matter of fact, Foremost Guernsey Association, Inc., operating Emmadine Farm, had the distinction of shipping a superbly bred Foremost Guernsey bull to England, which was as far as we know the first Guernsey to have been shipped from the United States *to* England. I recall another

Guernsey which we sent out to Turkey, and Foremost Guernsey blood lines have come to be well represented also in Canadian and Central American herds.

In a sense, through our work with Foremost blood lines, we have been spreading what amounts to a gospel, namely, that no herd ever can become great unless proper consideration is given to the bottom of the pedigree as well as to the top. A point coming more and more to be understood is that any and all work which benefits the individual herd constructively cannot but be reflected in betterment of the breed as a whole. When speaking of fanning out from Emmadine, as it were, and assembling a group of farms, severally devoting them to Guernseys and, for certain intervals, to Aberdeen Angus and Herefords besides fine horses, hogs and sheep, I like to emphasize that this bettering of livestock was no more a hobby with me than my mercantile business. My interest in the farms and their continuity of work has been an interest in a business, not merely a hobby, and has reflected my fundamental ideas of service, and profit-sharing as those ideas have dominated my mercantile business. Each farm has had to "stand on its own feet" and make money for us, not for money's sake but as a natural result of service which is of benefit to others. We have trained a great many young men, and it was a source of immense satisfaction to us all that, in the interest of helping to supply our boys overseas with good milk during World War II, Foremost activities spread around the world. This, to me, was a practical application in a very real sense of the Golden Rule. Although Foremost ranks statistically now as the third largest producers and distributors of dairy products in the world, the complex details of our round-the-world operation put a spirit of service before money.

Returning for a moment to the point of endowing herds, I would wish that other men might be moved to acquire and develop herds on the same principle, setting them up in perpetuity so that, after they pass out of their hands, valuable work may not be scattered, but conserved and carried forward uninterrupted. Such plans are an eloquent demonstration of two high aims which, though specifically attributed to Rotary, surely are susceptible of universal application: "He profits most who serves best" and "Service above Self."

About ten years ago I decided it would be better to see the work transferred while I was alive, and so the gift of the farm and herd was made available about three years later to the University at Columbia, Missouri.

In many ways this practical venture in agriculture and stock breeding has simply represented the adaptation in different terms of the principles and policies expressed in the company of men and stores. Occasions arise, just as frequently in the raising of purebred cattle as in any other line of endeavor, for a man to ask himself in his dealings with people, "Is this course right? Is it fair? Is it just?"

In the years of this venture, human interest stories have been legion which prove my point that where the desire to serve is present, success will come. I frequently recall the obstinacy of principle behind the experiences of a Polish youth with a purebred Guernsey cow; when I encountered him in 1926 they had led him about everywhere except to the poor house, and even that seemed a possibility.

August Johanik and I shared something of a kinship. Our families were poor, and were well acquainted with the same struggles to turn land to productivity. August's Polish parents had moved in 1909 from the Pennsylvania coal fields to a Slovak settlement in Wisconsin.

By the time he was eighteen August had to serve as head of the family. He got together a nice little show herd; the future looked promising until blackleg developed. Nine head died. August wouldn't accept defeat. He put a crushing price into purchase of a heifer, which proved a runt, which died at about the moment he finished paying for it.

Failures multiplied but he managed to buy another purebred heifer; Mary's Pride of White Plains became the nucleus of a purebred herd. What should happen but that his barn and silo burned. He had enough insurance to build a new foundation but he was deep in debt; and as for taxes! There were days when he had a choice; to buy a sack of flour, or a bag of feed for the cows. Neighbors were generous with advice: "You're crazy to try to hang on!"

His purebred cow was entered in the National Guernsey Sale, and it was there that I met him. He could think of nothing but that she might bring $500, enough to ease some of the debts.

She was knocked down for $2100. I was the successful bidder. Someone saw him crying, off by himself, for it meant the loss of a beauty. A lot of himself had gone into raising her.

She was worth every penny paid for her. She was more than a great animal; she was a symbol of what both August and I know is a great calling. Because of it, August was one of those many who didn't know how to quit.

It is incidents such as these that put men—and boys—into lifelong work with one breed or another. From the days when I had Aberdeen-Angus I well remember a boy, then in his teens, who sold me a steer he had raised. I paid eight dollars a pound, and it fetched the young man between $8000 and $9000, the highest price ever paid at that time for one of the breed.

The point is that it put the boy in the purebred Angus business for good. Everybody who knows anything about Angus breeders knows about Elliott Brown.

I am always elated when I observe young people, both boys and girls, for example, of the Future Farmers of America and the 4-H Clubs, beginning to get into one aspect or another of the enormously fascinating work of improving the quality of beef and dairy animals. Many of them were born on farms, of course; they have a real feeling for the work and would never think of going into anything else. Yet every once in a while one comes across a boy or girl who, without reference to background or upbringing, for some inner reason simply seems to have a natural bent for it. Occasionally it will puzzle a parent that a boy or girl, comfortably pointed in the direction of liberal arts education or one of the professions, has seemed to "fly off at a tangent" into agricultural college, with an interest in the breeding of livestock. It doesn't seem at all a tangent to me, but rather an important form of creative work.

Agriculture and the rearing of livestock as a means of livelihood are co-existent with the human race. Adam, having been thrust from the Garden of Eden under stern decree to earn his keep "by the sweat of his face" engaged in both; what he learned about these pursuits he handed on to Abel his son, who became "a keeper of sheep." Back in days when humankind was young, and for a long time afterward, a man's position in life—perhaps this is the real origin of the now much-discussed "status"—was determined by the size of his herds and flocks. Of course, the people of those early times were, in the main, pastoral in their mode of life, dependent upon cattle and other animals for daily subsistence. But down through time the life of man has been associated so closely with domestic creatures of various kinds, that it is well said that he cannot live without them.

It has been a matter of great pleasure and interest to me to observe one common bond, among others, between the successful men in the company, and the successful men on the farms. They are, alike, incurable optimists. I might say that they have to be—or they would bog down in the puzzlers that arise. They are not prone to wishful thinking or idle day dreams. They are steeped in what has been accomplished in the past; it is their lodestar, pointing the way to what may be done in the future.

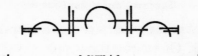

CHAPTER IX

Competition Through Service

Service is a prime instrument of competition. One of the great signs of our business times is that competition is keener but cleaner. The old cut-throat type of competition has diminished and we find competitors making common cause at many points, in United Fund and other health and social drives, and in Chamber of Commerce and fraternal organization campaigns.

I believe in vigorous competition in business and have often expressed the conviction that the best friend a progressive merchant can have is a fair competitor. I would broaden that and say that we benefit any life situation and ourselves through competition. There isn't much zest, after all, to rowing in slack water. The opportunities are big enough for all, and we do not need to fear competing for them. We should remind ourselves that our free-market tradition has endured in spite of cutthroat competition, not because of it.

Changes in thinking tend to come slowly. I remember that it came hard to a young man in one of our stores, for he had been harboring the old-fashioned theory that competition is synonymous with jealousy, aggressive hostility, and no-holds-barred fighting.

We received frantic word at the home office from him that a store of a different chain was going to open beside his own. All that stood in the way was the signing of the lease. Both stores would have the same landlord and what he wanted us to do as quickly as possible was to use our influence with the landlord to prevent the signing of the new lease.

"On the contrary," we sent back word, "we will do all we can to influence their getting the lease. They'll be excellent neighbors, good competitors. They will bring us more business and, if you work hard and fairly, you'll find you get your share." It turned out just as we anticipated, and everybody gained from the situation.

Robert Frost has said something which is apropos. "The beauty of life lies in the struggle, and change, and making tough decisions." I like to think that our young associate found things both more rewarding and interesting in a variety of ways, once he changed his thinking and welcomed competition on a different basis.

We have had many instances that were somewhat similar. I remember one ambitious store manager who sent us a hurry call for help with his advertising because a competitor was about to open a store in his vicinity. He had made a variety of plans. With the special advertising, he said, "We'll blast them with the kind of competition they've run into!" He disclosed further that, whereas the new store would close on opening day at the usual hour of 6 P.M., he was arranging to stay open until 10 P.M. "They'll never forget the reception we give them," he assured us. We lost no time in doing our part toward changing his thinking.

"Congratulations on having a new competitor!" we told him. "Thank your lucky stars for him. The more stores, the more business, remember!

"As you request, we are sending you advertising help. This will be the heading for your space advertising: Welcome to Homeville, R.H. & Company! We're glad you'll be with us!"

We added the further thought, "Incidentally, you will wish, we feel sure, to reconsider staying open later than your competitor, on the evening of his opening day. Not only would that put your store in the light of a bad neighbor and unfriendly competitor, it would fail of your purpose because you, by being open, would be going it alone, without your neighbor-stores to bring you customer traffic.

"Bear in mind, there will never be any better friend to a merchant than a fair competitor."

I am happy to recall the postscript to the incident. Being the kind of young man basically always ready to learn, he grasped the opportunity to be his own pacemaker. He had reacted impulsively on the old-fashioned concept that in any given area there is only a limited amount of business and that additional stores mean that the share of each will be cut that much thinner. His innate commonsense and intelligence led him around to the truth, that if a man does a good job, competition will be his friend instead of his enemy; however much competition there is, a merchant who approaches business with the determination to serve the public, will find business enough to go round.

The element of competition for business has always struck

me as a sort of plant food, a healthy nutrient stimulating the roots of enterprise and putting out new shoots of vigorous growth.

Let me draw an imaginary sketch. Picture any typical American street with the stores of its business district running along both sides of a main street. It you think about it you will probably discern two types of establishments, those which exude a spirit of a going business, and those that seem to have lost the zest for doing the things that attract and invite customers. Overall business in the locality seems to have settled at a certain jogging level.

But then into the scene comes a new store, run by an alert, trained merchant. He sets up in a store which looks, as the saying goes, smart as paint. Fixtures are attractive, lighting is good, the system of handling sales is efficient; windows are bright with colorful displays of merchandise, shown to best advantage. Advertisements are cast in lively, informative copy.

Is the reaction of neighboring merchants hostile and suspicious? Is the newcomer trying to "show them up"? Or is their reaction thoughtful and, in terms of their own enterprise, creatively competitive? I imagine the latter. A good example can work very contagiously.

A healthy sign that business has come of age regarding the factor of competition is found in the prevailing climate among merchants. In days when I worked in Hamilton for the Hales I would never have thought of entering the store of a competitor—it would have been frowned on by both sides. On the one hand, I might have been regarded as a traitor; on the other hand, as a spy.

Once, no one questioned that business had to be done on the basis of *caveat emptor*. Today no responsible merchant would dream of such a policy. The relationship of merchant and customer has become altogether different. The wise, enlightened and practical merchant knows that, like General Electric's slogan "Progress is our most important product," his most valuable stock in trade is Service. The customer is not a faceless someone, entering the store to part with X-number of dollars for something he needs or wants. He or she is, rather, a potential of mutual confidence. The reason that Service is the prime instrument of business competition is that, sincerely used, it relieves all concerned of the destructive nuisance of being wary!

Competition takes many forms. Underselling is the laziest and certainly not the most important of them. When competition is made creative it brings into being new and better ways of doing business, a fact on which there is no copyright.

In days when I came to market with Callahan and Johnson, they taught me that, before I went near a wholesaler to buy stock, I should "shop the windows." The theory being—and an enlightened and practical one it was—that, when you impressed people with your window displays, they would want to come in and buy.

Once this fact is grasped it may seem that it would be easy to avoid errors of judgment. Not always so. I recall an incident in one of our stores. The manager had bought from a retailer a few suits of a prestige brand, displaying them in his window at prices which would surprise customers and cause them to come in to buy. The suits were all small sizes.

Customers came in on the run, all right—to be brought up short by the fact that in most cases their size was not available. Through careless thinking the store manager was undermining our policy with a deception. He learned a useful lesson, namely, that the merchant who prepares to *fool* his customers into the store, first of all fools himself. In this case, the man brought about his own discharge.

When I hear people complaining that there is only just so much business to be had, and they have to fight any way they can to get their share, I like to remember Henry Ford. In a sense we started out in rather the same way. He too was a farmer's son. He left the farm to be an apprentice in a machine shop; I left it to sell dry goods. He borrowed $10,000 to get started; I borrowed $1500 for the same purpose. Both of us had in mind a service we could render to the middle class. My idea was to serve them with the best possible dollar's worth of service and quality in dry goods, and Mr. Ford's to serve them with the best possible dollar's worth of transportation for work and pleasure.

For many years I had the idea that I would like to meet him. I had the impression that we had a number of ideas in common. Unexpectedly it came about in 1943 that we met.

I happened to be on a store visit in Savannah. Our manager remarked in the course of conversation that, at the moment, Henry Ford was at his plantation there. Approaching him was described to me as a complicated and difficult affair, so I dismissed the idea from my mind, finding time however to pay a brief visit to that part of the plantation which at certain times was open to the public.

A day or two later my attention was called to an automobile parked across the street. "That's Mr. Ford's car; he has an office in that building." I thought nothing more of it until a telephone call came. If Mr. Penney could spare the time,

Mr. Ford would like to meet him. We conversed about many subjects. Naturally his philosophies on production and distribution methods were of great interest to me. We were in accord that serving the public well is of first importance, a determining factor in success.

For this and allied reasons, I don't put any great stock in the mounting refrain that the little fellow no longer has a chance and can't meet the competition.

There couldn't have been a littler "little fellow" than I, when I started out with my first store. I can hear some readers say, "Oh, but in 1902 things were different than they are now, nearly sixty years later."

True—up to a point. Community needs have grown along with the size and complexity of business. But in the early days we certainly had as many problems proportionately as business has today. Now, as then, I believe that any "little fellow" who studies the needs and will work hard to serve them, already has his chance, and it is for him to say what he will do with it, make of it.

Now and then I meet people who assume, from the size and strength of the Penney Company, that it has met and overcome all its competition. I wouldn't look at it that way at all, nor would I like to see it happen. In any human situation competition is and should be the constant star. Competition is no enemy, it is an ally, and when translated in service, it is a constant spur to betterment through more service and thus benefits all.

It is in the make-up of human beings that they need incentive. In this connection I am reminded that, in 1778, when his officers and men were resigning in wholesale numbers because of economic pressures, George Washington wrote a friend, "Men may talk of patriotism, they may point to great achievements performed by its influence, but it alone is not a sufficient basis for conducting a long and bloody war. I do not exclude the idea of patriotism, but a great and lasting war must be aided by a prospect of interest, or some reward. Patriotism may, of itself, push men to action, to bear much, to encounter difficulties, but it will not endure unless assisted by reward." I believe that these words proceeded out of a penetrating wisdom, that behind them was the practical knowledge that men *need* the incentive of individual rewards. In my selections of men, on the basis of the particular attributes we were looking for in relation to the spirit of our way of doing business, as soon as they began to get responsibility they also began to feel that they were in business for themselves. I am not very happy at seeing government getting into people's lives, by way of controls and limitations on incentives and enterprise. From our early beginnings, through our profit-sharing system a man was in effect put into business for himself because of the share he had in profits which he helped to create. As George Washington indicated, this supplied the "prospect of interest, or reward."

Is there not here a practical thought-provoker for today, in light of the fact that the core of our still valuable competitive enterprise system is the inherent human desire for interest and reward? All have in common the desire to get ahead, and need the incentive of material benefits and commensurate recognition when we succeed. It has been our experience that a man will feel a spontaneous allegiance for a company which takes the natural desires of the human spirit into account and designs the way for them to be realized. I have sometimes been asked whether, as our original plan evolved, taking on supplemental aspects, the direction didn't tend toward paternalism. Nothing could be farther from the fact. Paternalization weakens people; putting them in position to reach the horizons of their own powers makes them free.

When I speak of the life-blood qualities of competition, of course I am not talking about the dog-eat-dog kind of struggle for a limited amount of business. To my mind that sort of thing is thoroughly *passé*. In its true and right form, competition is a creative force, not gobbling up, leaving the next man with nothing in sight to accomplish, but a force which activates business, and supplies momentum. I believe wholeheartedly that literally there is no limit of opportunity for exercising incentive. It follows, that where incentive produces some commodity or service that people need and want, there opportunity will be, to do business and succeed.

Except that obviously it was the serious decision of a mature man, I am tempted to laugh at the poor fellow who, a hundred years ago, resigned his job in the U.S. Patent Office, explaining that everything had been patented, and consequently there was no more work for him there. As the Patent Office had only existed twenty-four years, what was really lacking was his own faith and vision, much as it is lacking in people who say that today there is no place any longer for the (so-called) "little fellow." There will always be a place for anyone with a good and practical idea, willing to work unstintingly to get it accepted and translated into terms of the service of practical use.

Parenthetically, apropos of the impulsive man who pulled out of his Patent Office employment, the other day I saw a statement from the Patent Office to the effect that "it is now giving the most prompt service to applications since the end of World War II. And with the time for obtaining a patent on something patentable now about a year and a half, our goal is for even more prompt service."

It is often mistakenly assumed that an invention, based on an idea for a service, is the last word on the subject. More often it is only the first "word" of a great many. I have in mind that classic article the "macintosh," developed by Charles Macintosh, a Scottish chemist and inventor, in 1823 when he produced a waterproof fabric to make an enveloping garment to wear in the rain. Macintoshes crossed the Atlantic and, proving adequate, sold everywhere for the purpose. By degrees people came along who asked themselves whether there was any good reason why a garment which would give protection against rain had to be quite so drab in appearance. Now we can trace back to Macintosh an enormous industry, turning out raincoats which are more like walking flower gardens or abstract paintings than any kin to Mr. Macintosh's concept of a protective garment to keep one warm and dry.

Free competition is a healthy stimulant to business, and friendly rivalry far more customary among businessmen today than self-defeating cutthroat tactics. In large cities and small towns where we have stores, it has happened repeatedly that the principal department store merchant *invited* us to come into the shopping district. In one store, an established, famously successful department store went a step farther, itself constructing a building directly across the street for us to lease. In another city the local department store, experiencing a slump in shopping traffic, divided its space in order to rent part of it to us for a Penney store. These people not only did not fear effects of free, fair competition, but they sought it out and welcomed it.

I like another episode because it shows that, though it is not necessarily easy always to meet competition, it can be done.

A town containing one of our stores is situated on a main road which leads to three large and busy shopping centers. It was inevitable—yet, as it turned out, not necessarily fatal—that when the shopping centers were opened, customers would by-pass continuing to buy at home, and travel to them. A pall of discouragement gathered over the home business section. One or two merchants gave up without delay.

Various remedies were explored. Could a concentrated appeal be made to people's home town loyalty? It was felt that, as considerable impetus enters into shopping habits, mere appeals would be rather nebulous. It began to look as though keeping people in town to shop would be a small miracle— if it could be brought about. The question was, How?

All the merchants in town got together in a meeting of the Retail Committee of the Chamber of Commerce, and set up a Home Bargain Day for each month. Each merchant pledged to offer only super values on that day. Each contributed his share to costs of a Gala monthly event—banners, streamers, advertising. The local newspaper cooperated enthusiastically by running a special edition, heavy with well-planned advertising, for distribution in outlying farming areas and small villages.

Each succeeding year gains of more than 100% over the preceding year are regular occurrances. Not only does business on Gala days show the effects, but there has been a general business upturn because this dramatization of the Shop-at-

Home habit brought into relief solid advantages of regular shopping there.

If it seems that I have dwelt at length on the element of competition in relation to interests of my own, let me emphasize my conviction that application of the spirit and values of competition are practically limitless.

Competition is a form of aspiration, and aspiration is an indivisible part of our fiber as Americans. Free competition has kept us and will always keep us from becoming a stagnant nation; without it business, large or small, would not survive, without it we as a nation would not survive. For example, the average farmer is a "little fellow," but can you separate his welfare from the welfare of the railroad which transports his seeds, his tools, or from the welfare of the manufacturer who makes his plow, the production line that produces his tractor, his pick-up truck, his family automobile? The average grocer is a "little fellow," but can you visualize where the great food producers would be without him—or he without them?

A few examples of this kind are surely enough to lay the ghost that there's no place any longer for the "little fellow," that he can't meet the competition.

As I have said, I believe that any merchant who approaches business with the determination first of all to serve the public well, has nothing to fear from competition. Deep in the human make-up is the need to meet an opposing element and succeed in the meeting. Competition, keener and cleaner today than ever before, supplies that need.

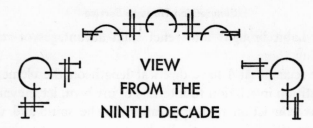

VIEW FROM THE NINTH DECADE

CHAPTER X

Starting Over at Fifty-six Is Possible

"Among all my patients in the second half of life . . . every one of them fell ill because he had lost what the living religions of every age have given their followers, and none of them has been really healed who did not regain his religion. . . ." This is the observation of the distinguished psychiatrist Professor C. G. Jung.

I can attest to its insight out of personal experience. Having chased Mammon pretty hard and far, at the age of fifty-six I was confronted by the fact that the only way I could survive was to start all over, spiritually and in business. I was bewildered and adrift. To begin again would be possible only if my whole thinking changed. That could only come with God's help.

I would not want it inferred that experiences of mine in lost moorings are unique, or fell harder on me than they could have on anyone else. I know many men who have reached great extremity. The point in common with the majority is the humbly frank recognition that the only way back lies "in the shadow of the Almighty."

My father had been to me living evidence that the Christian way is meant to pervade and direct every thought, word, act and relationship of life. His labor on the farm—plowing, sowing, reaping, stock-raising—was as sacred to his way of thinking as was his calling to preach the Word of God. Every obligation, in no matter what category, was to him a clear-cut spiritual responsibility; each was to be performed faithfully, as part and parcel of the Lord's work. In teaching this attitude to me, he bestowed a rich spiritual capital. Further he impressed on me that a man can be a true and faithful Christian, and at the same time carry on his business or profession. There was a prevailing scepticism on the point, but my father never questioned that a man could combine the two without compromising either—if he would.

From the time I opened the first store in Kemmerer, in 1902, I tried consistently to apply the Christian principle of the Golden Rule in all dealings, with the public on the opposite side of the counter, with our clerks on our side. Every single day I learned more of the truth that the only chance for the real worth and power of this and all other Christian principles to emerge lies in what *we* do with them. The power of any principle, ethical, intellectual, spiritual, material, can work only as it is brought out in the open by *action*. My own experience with the Golden Rule long since convinced me that it is, to the business organization or individual who will translate it into action, what a ship's compass is to the mariner. It is the perfectly calibrated instrument, always pointing out the right direction.

As I recall many pitfalls I encountered, and hazards which threatened me along the way, I am conscious of the sublime assurance that *He* never forsook me. This I must acknowledge, not only where business matters were concerned, but also in things of more personal nature. Sad to say, at many points my gratitude took only the form of passive gestures amid all-round living. Because I want to bear humble witness to His patience, and with the thought that others—especially any who may not be walking closely with God—may derive some benefit from my experience, I share here parts of an intimate and sacred episode in my life.

In the early 1930s I was overtaken by almost total financial disaster. It was a period in which many people became caught in large forces. As money had become—I thought—my strength, so, in a circuitous way, had it become my undoing.

Early in my business career I had an ambition to be worth $100,000; that, I told myself, would surely be enough for any man. Soon however—as had my desire to have twenty-five stores and then quit, changed by degrees to fifty stores, then one hundred, then more and more—so my interest in amassing money no longer stopped at $100,000. Then I wanted $1,000,-000. "Then," I would stop. But "then" the chase became too exciting, too absorbing.

I didn't feel myself "money mad" because, simultaneously, I was developing systematic giving of my means to philanthropic needs where I felt a sympathy with objectives and thought I could be of help.

There is a natural aversion to "conscience giving," which is really no giving at all. There will never be any dearth of good and useful causes. One wishes to develop a sound philosophy of giving which will be individual and become creative.

Again, Dr. Short was very helpful, leading my thinking in this direction. Never making up my mind for me—he would have drawn back from that as quickly as I—he increased my awareness of the connection between the experiencing of God's power in one's life, and the privileges of giving.

The best "conduit" for what I had in mind seemingly would be some type of foundation. I had in mind an approach which would *relate people to people* for the beneficial working out of concrete problems, and a foundation could be carefully designed to implement it. My longtime observation is that successful answers to problems come in the form of human beings, not in elaborate, academic blueprints.

At a public dinner I had met Dr. Daniel A. Poling, then pastor (now associate minister) of Marble Collegiate Church at Fifth Avenue and West 29th Street in New York. He had made a strong impression on me; among other things he was a militant defender of the younger generation and, in character and temperament, a born youth leader.

In about 1926 therefore, I had explained to Dr. Poling my intentions regarding a J. C. Penney Foundation and asked him to be its Director. There would be no connection whatever between it and the J. C. Penney Company except that in one form and another both reflected my personal conviction and experiences with the practice of Christian principles in all life situations. The diversified interests I intended to give to through the Foundation were selected personally, undertaken on my own initiative and solely at my expense. They ranged then from an aspect of vocational guidance, expressed through the National Youth Radio Conference, of which Dr. Poling was the leader, to Penney Farms and the Memorial Home Community in Clay County, Florida, the *Christian Herald,* the monthly magazine so immensely valuable to Protestantism on a truly interdenominational basis, and other projects.

Of course, my main interest continued to be the Company. But I was now of a mind and in a position to pour large sums into the Foundation for these new purposes, using my personal shares in the company as collateral for bank borrowings.

At about the same time, catching interest in Florida from the late Carl Fisher and others, I followed up a conviction that Miami and its surrounding region had a tremendous future and that, in 1926–27 what it needed most was friends, who would believe the area had a future and act accordingly.

The purposes in which I involved myself and my support were in themselves right and good. I could not bear to cut back on any of them. Finally external forces combined to sweep away the bulk of my personal holdings and I came to a complete stop. To lose money is one thing; to have motives questioned is another, and harder to bear.

"Experience is not what happens to one, it is what one does with what happens." It was some time before I could get any perspective on my mistakes. I rationalized that, because the things I wanted money to do were good and necessary, I had done nothing that was wrong. More and more money had been needed in order to help others. I grew more and more blind to the degree to which I had allowed the idea of possessing huge sums of money to possess me.

This self-justification was pathetically blind. My reasoning took no account of self-deception, false pride, lack of humility. I had told myself that wealth made a man invincible, invulnerable against attack even of economic forces. I had to learn that I had been attacked first by my own self-esteem, pride and material ambition. Now, through the working of inexorable law—"What shall it profit a man, if he gain the whole world, and lose his own soul?"—I saw everything tangible swept away.

One must feel shamed at having to turn to God because there is nothing else left. Yet, like all people who first must take time to blame others for disaster brought on by no fault except their own, it took time for me to find the grace to make the turn.

Like an animal that is crippled, I hid away, as much from myself as from the limelight and legal difficulties. About four years previous the present Mrs. Penney and I had been married in Paris. We closed off all but two or three rooms at Whitehaven, let the servants go, and lived there in a stunned abeyance.

As I look back on it all I can still feel astonished as well as mortified at having got so far away, not only from first principles but from innate habit. I had always been a fighter, thriving on obstacles; now I felt beaten, cowering. Time dragged. I wandered the grounds, seeing enemies lurking behind every bush. Unwittingly making use of manual therapy, I cut brush, picked up fieldstones, pulled weeds. How often had I watched my father pull the weeds that marred his beloved bluegrass! I was not following his example of faith in God, yet I hardly gave it a thought. Dimly I knew that he would tell me now, if he could, to stop whimpering, to look my downfall in the face for what it was—something not unconnected with certain external forces yet, in the last analysis, a thing of my own doing, *and certainly not irreparable.*

It is a sidelight on that point in the experience that I became aware, as I think I had never been, of the marvel which is one's hands. I believe there were times when using my hands, my fingers, saved my reason.

Slowly, fearfully, I began asking myself, What, after all, has *really* happened to me? Well, I had lost some money, quite a good deal, in fact. But what else had I *lost, really* lost?

Nothing—nothing, that is, that counted. I had lost pride and vanity, the sense of being invincible. But I had lost none of the faculties, the abilities with which I had begun to build, at Kemmerer, and which I still had. Plenty of men had started over. Who was to say I would remain permanently beaten— unless, of course, it were myself?

My distracted mind caught hold of these threads and began working, rather fearfully, but working nevertheless. Now tormented by bitterness and resentment, now grasping at the threads and trying to derive from them some equilibrium, I kept on going through motions; I sorted stones for a strip of dry wall, felled an oak sapling attacked by blight. I conjured up the guilty irony that I too had been blighted, but was too absorbed in inertia to more than half-heartedly rebuke my self-pity.

Self-pity becomes a sort of film over the spirit. What I needed was for my spiritual sight to be restored—only how? From time to time, without being bidden, verses from Scripture came back to me. ". . . For thus saith the Lord God . . . In returning and rest shall ye be saved, and in confidence shall be your strength. . . . But ye would not. . . ." It didn't seem to take hold. I had been strong— money had made me so—and the money was gone—— Another day, hefting a stone, I paused to watch a bluejay as it flew screeching overhead, and settled on a pine branch. ". . . . the cedars of Lebanon, which He hath planted, where the birds make their nests. . . ." I watched the bird, first use the branch like a trampoline and then, with a bold screech, take flight in a flash of blue plumage. I thought of God's out-of-doors and realized that for a long time I had merely taken it for granted.

I do not imply that in a blinding flash a way back to solid ground opened miraculously before me or that, even by halt-ing steps, I was lifted quickly out of despair. The process was neither easy nor short.

Long ahead, I had made certain store visitation and speak-ing engagements. A mocking question posed itself. What could I have to say now that would have any meaning or usefulness? Besides, I felt too ill to do what would be expected of me; I had convinced myself that friends, even family, had accepted my failure, and drawn away from me.

Habit is strong. I went to keep my engagements. As it happened one of them was at Battle Creek. A bit wry: *Battle Creek.*

When I had fulfilled my speaking obligation, with great inadequacy, I felt sure, I asked one of the doctors at the sanitarium—an old schoolmate in Hamilton, Dr. Elmert Eg-gleston—to examine me.

"Jim," he said to me frankly, "I don't like what I find. We'll have to get you some relief from this mental and emotional shock." He was calm, assured. He put me to bed, assigned round-the-clock nurses, and I wondered helplessly if he would believe me if I were to tell him I didn't have the money to pay for this much attention.

I wanted to refuse sedatives; I had always had an instinctive aversion to them. But first I must have some rest——

There's nowhere for me to turn but to God, I had told

myself over and over again. Yet what had I done about it? Nothing. I had not prayed. I could not honestly say I had even tried to pray.

I grew rested enough to insist—convincingly, I hoped—that the three shifts of nurses were unnecessary. The doctor studied me. He knew me well, and I think divined my reason. But he authorized a change to routine nursing care—on condition that I stay on sedatives. I was making poor headway, I knew; so harassed was my mind that unless I obtained more relief, rest, I could not hope to attack my obligations——

". . . be clothed with humility, for God resisteth the proud and giveth grace to the humble. . . . Humble yourselves therefore under the mighty hand of God . . . casting all your care upon Him, for He careth for you. . . ."

It is strange, how in the midst of weakness we can be so strong in resisting God's help; how we can cling to the blindness of our own stubborn way.

One evening I felt a clear and peculiar awareness, that when the morning came, my life would have ended. A curious, detached precision took hold of me. In the early part of the evening they brought me the usual sedative, and I slept a while; when I woke up about nine o'clock, it was like picking up a book to finish a chapter.

It did not enter my mind to demand a reprieve, to marshal my forces in order to still do things in the world that I wanted to do. I accepted the idea that it was now out of my hands. Getting out of bed I sat at the desk for some time, writing farewell letters to my family and two or three close friends. In a twilight state of detached calm, I went back to bed and slept.

Shortly after dawn I awoke. I felt no joy at being alive,

saw no omen of hope, experienced nothing more than mere consciousness. But then a faint wonderment entered my mind. Feeling apprehensive yet restless, abstractedly I dressed and went downstrairs, with some vague idea that I would eat breakfast.

The dining room doors were not open; I wandered along a corridor, with no conscious direction. I became aware of a thread of music. I turned my ear to it and recognized an old familiar hymn.

> God will take care of you. . . . Through every day,
> o'er all the way. . . . He will give peace to your aching
> heart, God will take care of you. . . . Lean, weary one,
> upon His breast, God will take care of you. . . . Be
> not dismayed, whate'er betide, God will take care of
> you. . . .

I followed in the direction of the sound. It was coming from the chapel. People had come there to begin the day with a prayer meeting. I went in and sat down in the back row.

I do not believe we can put the inmost reactions at such times into words, nor, perhaps, are we meant to. *Miracle* seems somehow a pale word for what happened to me, in a space of about twelve hours. Suddenly needing to be heard I cried inwardly, "Lord, will *You* take care of me? I can do nothing for myself!" As though I had been pinned to earth up till then by an intolerable weight, I felt the burden lifting from my body and spirit. I sat there, scarcely daring to breathe. I felt I was passing out of darkness into light. "Only believe!" the Bible tells us. "Only believe." In the midst of failure to believe, I was being helped back to believing. I could hardly credit what seemed to be happening to me, but this much I could sense: in His compassion and boundless love, God was stretching out His hand to lift me up from the welter of confusion and misery, as I had been taught by my parents that He would, setting me on my feet again, bidding me pick up my life, this time "in the shadow of the Almighty."

The reader will know now, why I was so interested in the statement by Dr. Jung, quoted at the beginning of this chapter. For a long time, while maintaining practice of my ethical beliefs, I had unconsciously substituted them for spiritual action. When circumstances overwhelmed me, wrong thinking caused me to become sick and despairing; my only chance to be healed lay in regaining my religion. Many steps had to be retraced, to find true causes; perhaps even the very financial losses were, in fact, a result of wrong thinking.

I had harbored the certainty that I would not live through a certain night. I know now that there is more than one kind of death. As I saw it with clearing vision, the episode in the chapel, known then only to God and myself, was in reality the death of the man I had been, and—joined closely with it, in a wondrous way—the birth of the man God wanted me to me. It marked my first consciousness of having touched the hem of His healing garment.

Now my first task, as I saw it, was with God's help to change my whole thinking. Although I had tried sincerely all of my business life to be guided explicitly by Christian principles, and though I had never gone on even a short trip without a Bible to read before going to bed, I had nevertheless failed to follow Christ's teachings personally as I should have. God had given me success far beyond my expectations, but I had not loved Him as I should have, and had shamefully neglected His church. Above all, I began now to realize, though I had regarded myself for thirty years as being in partnership with God, I had supported His cause by giving money only, when I should first have been giving of myself.

Revolving these things in my mind, another attitude of life altogether began opening ahead of me. God was giving me another chance. Something Dr. Short had said to me in the latter months of his lifetime came back to me with particular meaning. "Penney, do you know what I think? Your greatest work is yet to come."

Such experiences have in one way or another come to many men. The change begun in me was so decisive to my health that I was able to resume my speaking itinerary and, two weeks after that morning prayer service in the chapel I was at home, celebrating Christmas with my family.

It began to seem to me that I had never before really lived. I was spiritually and mentally refreshed, ready for positive steps. I approached prayer from an entirely new direction, the means of bringing me into that intimate relationship with God wherein His will can be revealed. I was baptized into church membership. Friends introduced me to the Layman's Movement and its work, and I learned of a prayer group of business and professional men, meeting in mid-town New York at the start of the business day, and joined with them.

"The one thing more needed" was to learn humbly how to give *myself personally* to God's purposes for my life. Taking my faith seriously I must seek and find His will for the use of the talents I had been endowed with, and the experiences through which I had passed. Literally, "Experience is what we do with what happens to us."

Instead of reading the Bible, I began to study it. Through study and sincere practice of prayer, I discovered what everyone may discover, if he will: prayer profoundly enlightens and alters one. Through prayer—"Thou wilt shew me the path of life; in thy presence is fullness of joy"—he is able to see himself more as he actually is; he can see his faults, his fears, his talents, his potentialities. Responsively he may move closer to wisdom and humility, to an awareness of his obligations, to God and to his fellowman. True prayer opens the eyes to things not seen before, the ears to things not heard before, in contrast to that prayer which has been the mere reflection of selfish desires, so colored by puny will that, only being endlessly repeated, it can bring no real answer.

For many years it had been part of my work as a merchant to speak on the general subject of Christian principles in business, to audiences of varying size and makeup in all parts of the United States and Canada. Now, influenced by my acquaintance with the Layman's Movement point of view, my speaking became a kind of evangelization in behalf of the inspiration, strength and guidance to be received through close reliance upon Christ and the positive practice of a creative Christianity. The altered perspective became the new beacon of my life.

It did not turn the problem of having to start all over again into anything magically easy, but in hard tasks I had new companions: genuine prayer, faith and trust, a sense of "God, from whom all blessings flow." Throughout grueling periods in law courts where great business and financial complications had to be adjudicated, I carried a slip of paper in my pocket, referring often to it: "He shall cover thee with His feathers, and under His wings shalt thou trust. His truth shall be thy shield and buckler. . . ."

Many times the advice of my father came back from his own dark hour to me. Driven from the church he loved and served, he never allowed his hurt to turn to bitterness, and he constantly urged me not to harbor bitterness toward those who had judged him. When I listened to lawyers, wrangling that lack of character and moral responsibility in me had brought severe financial loss to others, or that I had sacrificed a bank in order to save myself, I could only hope to face what I knew to be untruths with the forebearance, of which the Savior's is the great example—"Father, forgive them, for they know not what they do"—and practiced by my father, as one of His humble followers.

By God's mercy and love, as I humbly came to see His plans for me, it was given to me to begin again. I discovered how wrong I had been in thinking I had been abandoned; my family was as loving and loyal as they had always been. Gradually I was enabled to recover much lost material ground. A younger brother and two friends each loaned me $50,000 without security, and I'm sure without asking themselves if they would ever be paid back.

"And seekest thou great things for thyself? Seek them not . . ." Jeremiah reminded Baruch, his helper. All I had lost really was money. Much, of course, never has, or could be, regained, yet I cannot mourn this too greatly because the circumstances led to my discovering too much of infinitely greater worth to take its place. The most immediate lesson in Christ's teachings is that there is no enduring happiness in *getting*, in *having*; happiness only comes in giving.

I did make money again in time, but from harsh experience I had learned a lesson in the value of money. Possession of money cannot guarantee invulnerability, and the power imputed to money cannot be relied on. On the contrary, the job well done, the inward joy in being of service—these are treasures that never can be taken away.

Every day I was to be given, in which to live and to share the discoveries and meanings of hard experience, was to become priceless.

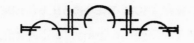

CHAPTER XI

The Disciplined Are Free

The topic of big business affects some people today rather like the sudden loosing of one of those nerve-stretching bolts of artificial lightning in a General Electric laboratory. However, I mention big business here for purposes of contrast, in connection with making a point which young people especially, with their careers ahead of them, might well consider.

Big business did not found the material substance and wealth of our country. It was begun by individualistic, rugged-minded, hard-working men, who started small. Making their way along hazardously, they accepted great risks with determined faith, under strong discipline—self-discipline.

The point I want to make is discipline. The disciplined are free.

I don't envy today's young people the availability of so much "security" which seemingly relieves them of the necessity, and the creative adventure of hard effort. The quickest, easiest short-cut to a shiny house, a big car, a big slice of leisure time—this objective disturbs me more for the elements it leaves out than for those it includes. "Status" and the four-day week are becoming more important than work and pride in it. Work and occupation is men's natural sphere. Discipline is a form of pride in work.

I do not like to see young people lulled by security to the point where there are no surprises to look forward to. A few surprises—even momentarily uncomfortable ones—never hurt any businessman made of the right stuff; his quality lies in turning them to advantage, and learning from them.

What do I mean when I hold that the disciplined are free? I mean that people who put themselves under the discipline of great principles and conscientious practices, go far in liberating themselves from the pitfalls of haphazard or inferior standards. They do not have to stop so often to patch up the road, so to speak, but can proceed straight ahead on a wide, way. Lack of discipline can be very costly in wasted time and effort. I often think of a remark made by the great evangelist, Dwight L. Moody: "I have never met a man who has given me as much trouble as myself."

That the disciplined are free is not a paradox. A disciplined life does not necessarily presuppose being hemmed in by all manner of restraints and those arbitrary limitations whose chief effect is to obstruct and annoy. The discipline of high standards can produce a revolving credit of spiritual contentment and spacious freedom of action. The Master of Discipline told His followers that the purpose of His teaching was "That your joy may be full."

If material human interests are to grow through the application of Christian principles it will require our growing in humility. Although it took me many years to grasp that my mother's frequent prayer, "Lord, be merciful to me, a sinner" was basic to her attitudes of religion, convictions, home and work, a simple heart-cry of humility, I realize now that humility is the strength of the relationship between all human beings.

The original context of that appeal to heaven—"Be merciful to me, a sinner"—shows us a strongly-contrasted pair, the Pharisee and the publican. The Pharisee prayed aloud, that all might take note of his piety. The other worshiper placed himself behind a pillar, directing his eyes at the ground while he prayed. Jesus may have been in the Temple Courts that day, and so have heard the whispered devotions of this humble man. His subsequent sermonette took note that "he that humbleth himself shall be exalted," and of "certain who trusted in themselves that they were righteous, and despised others . . ." The parable was directed against excessive self-esteem and self-righteousness. It emphasizes that humility is the central virtue in an adequate relationship to God. And it is implicit in the Golden Rule.

It strikes me that we still lag behind on recognizing that being "in favor with God and man" is the surest foundation for success in whatever category. So far from there being anything weak or abject about this virtue, it is the sterling-mark of the man wise enough not to trust in himself or his own righteousness; it is certainly visible in the man who never makes the mistake of looking down on others.

In business we are very conscious, of course, of making provisions for audits, stocktaking, periodic taking of inventory. I suggest that self-examination is as important in the life of the individual. Clearly, if we are to benefit from such action, we must not be blinded by pride and self-esteem. We must begin in the company of the publican rather than of the Pharisee; we must emulate the publican's spirit, pray his prayer.

"Know thyself" was advice offered by the Greek poet Menander before the time of Christ. Many thinkers and writers have extended and adapted the thought, one among them commenting, "In many ways the saying 'Know thyself' is not well said. It were more practical to say 'Know other people.' " It is sound common sense to practice either or both. The man who acquaints himself with both his weak and his strong points is likely to approach other men in a spirit which will set an example as well as engender confidence and good will; in this way he will be exemplifying the basic relationship conveyed in the Golden Rule.

In my own business career, the recommendation to "Know other people" has taken the form of selecting men not solely because they had certain business abilities but because they believe in a Supreme Being and discipline themselves to high moral and related standards. I cannot regard the spirit of men as an extra.

Without imputing sainthood to them, I see many business-men—both leaders and rank-and-file—whose motivation deserves to be called a vocation because it is palpably based on an energizing belief in God and a humble consciousness of self-limitation. Herein, I believe, are the roots of service which, as I have said, is to my mind the first element of success. Even though it may manage to show money profits, business which does not grow out of *offering service* is, I believe, a failure.

Discipline, not indulgence, will get things done. Perhaps I

might illustrate the "look of discipline," or lack of it, by a small incident observed in one of the stores.

A customer came up to the counter and asked to see a men's shirt of a certain size and color. The clerk took a shirt from the shelf and dropped it on the counter. "Isn't that a nice shirt?" he said. His gaze wandered away from the customer and he waited; evidently to his mind the sale would be made, or it would not, and that was all there was to it.

As it happened, the sale was made. I took the opportunity to ask the sales clerk some questions. "How long have you been selling shirts?" I inquired.

"All my life," he said cheerfully.

Did he like selling shirts? Was there anything he would like selling better? Shirts were fine, yes, he liked selling them; no, there was nothing he knew of that he'd like selling better.

"If you'll show me one of the shirts of the type you just sold your customer," I said, "perhaps I can make a suggestion."

Looking a little surprised, but interested, he got down the shirt.

"Did you notice that this material is woven madras?" I said. "A fine shirting. And notice how the shirt is full cut. As you see, there is fine stitching, the quality of the pearl buttons excellent." He looked at me affably, still interested; but I had an idea that what he was saying inside was, "So?" It hadn't taken any palavering to sell the shirt.

"You'll make better sales and your own work more interesting, too, I believe, if you *tell* them those things."

He studied me for a minute. Then a smile broke over his face.

"I see what you mean," he said. "Service and sales, both."

"You've got the idea," I said. Now he would be freer for

the discipline—self-learned—of a higher standard of performance.

We gain in the long run by denying ourselves the easy way.
It is not the challenges that are fewer; what is wanting is more
people to go out and meet them head-on. The astronauts, a
company of disciplined young men, are disciplining themselves
more every day against the time when they will go out to
meet and compete with the secrets of outer space. I like to
think that in terms of their own work in the world they are
meeting the call of the Savior of men who said a hard thing
when He urged "If any man will come after Me, let him deny
himself, and take up his cross and follow Me." These young
men are by-passing the easy way, casting their lot with the
power and disciplines of accepting the difficult way. In the
ultimate sense, each of these young men will one day be alone
with the inner power which God gives to handle the hard task.
The knowledge that the Creator is a co-partner never can rule
out the necessity for personal discipline and hard work. Surely
the strict meaning of self-reliance is disciplined confidence
in God-given abilities and unwavering determination to use
them. Time has to be regarded as divinely-provided opportunity to be used carefully, one might even say reverently.

Follow through with me in this logical order. Another facet
of discipleship—for the disciplined life means discipleship—
is self-control. What unpleasant people we can be without the
vital and formative lessons of early years! Children and teenagers often rebel against the curbs and controls of early re-
stricted life and are slow to see their characters as in the
molding process. All of us learn—some more easily than
others—that no man or boy, no woman or girl, lives alone;
that what each does and says and even thinks will somehow

affect the lives of others. The most obvious sign of lack of discipline is selfishness; selfishness may successfully pilfer sister's favorite hair-ribbon or ski mittens but it will not build sisterly harmony. Selfishness sometimes wins momentary material gains but the rewards that come through service will last longer and be more satisfying all around.

Nowadays numerous voices are blaming juvenile delinquency on comics, sub-standard books, television and even radio. It is conceivable that, with their substantial emphasis on violence and disorder, they do contribute to social problems. But for the main cause ought we not to go to the root of the matter, and look in the direction of parents?

Self-expression is excellent when maintained within the gentle confines of the greater good of the family and society; when children, or adults for that matter, forget this, society is threatened. Perhaps the chief form of threat comes in the interpretation of liberty as freedom to say and do whatever the individual likes, no matter how disturbing to others. A wise man said, "True liberty is freedom *to do what you ought to do.*" President Eisenhower has pinpointed this by saying, "Liberty is the priceless opportunity for self-discipline." No family, association of men, or culture can function effectively unless they subscribe to certain codes of conduct. Discipline begins when individuals—first alone, then collectively—subscribe to such codes. From the Creator's fashioning of this earth and the beginning of time there have been such codes, expressed in differing forms. All agree basically that man has certain rights, but that they are possessed within the relationships of men to his Maker, and his neighbors. If he forgets his Creator, and ignores his duties in relation to his fellowman, he is in turn untrue to himself.

We must admit in general that observation shows man to be a self-centered being. William Gladstone, the great British statesman, pointed out that "Selfishness is the greatest curse of the human race." Perhaps we would get the point more positively if we set ourselves to visualize a way of life *in which unselfishness rules*. Certainly we can realize by now that, if any world-changing in the spiritual sense is to come, the starting-point lies with the individual.

If we truly desire to enjoy freedom we cannot evade individual responsibility, and can only have it in proportion as we exert the discipline freedom requires. Self-examination, self-control, and self-denial are not qualities which, once acquired, will look after themselves. Requiring constant conserving and renewal, God's power must be added to sustain them.

If it is true, and I firmly believe it is, that there is no right dividing line between the business and the Christian, or religious, way of life, then there is every practical as well as moral and spiritual reason to strive toward a new personal relationship with God. The doorway to contact with that source of all life is unpretentious, the only card of admission needed "a humble and a contrite heart." Humbleness has been defined as "a perpetual quietness of heart." I am reminded of it, for example, whenever I recall a daily prayer meeting led by one of the Red Caps in a quiet part of the Grand Central Station in New York. This is a kind of self-renewal and, if we possess the discipline and humbleness to seek and apply it, is available to us all.

I can make no claim to having attained heights of spiritual perception or action, but I should like to think that, in the lights and shadows of a long business career and life, I have absorbed useful ideas which might spur others to make greater use of God's gifts to them. Through experience I learned that, to be free, one must follow; to gain success one must serve. I am a practical man and I know, on the practical side, that there are greater opportunities today than ever before in this country and, for that mattter, the world over. I am rather sorry when I see our colleges making what seems to me the mistake of training young people to sell their services on the basis of the highest price. Except that one should have sufficient to live comfortably, I think the tests and adventure come with putting money second and opportunities for the future first. As I have said earlier, for young people who are thoroughly honest, willing to make sacrifices if necessary, the opportunities are already there, and the money will come. This order of things requires disciplined mind and spirit. From it stems a positive kind of liberty, useful to the world as well as to the individual. And so, for young people first but really for all people, I covet the courage and impulse to look into one's own heart with sincerity; to look outward in service to one's fellowmen; to look upward to God in joyous discipline and surrender.

CHAPTER XII

Prayer, A Business Companion

I have no difficulty in recalling times when a businessman
who talked openly about the use of prayer would have been
regarded by many people as eccentric to say the least. It is one
of the positive gains of our times that it is no secret that many
influential men rely frankly on seeking God's guidance for
enlightened understanding, and the kind of decisions which,
because of their positions of responsibility and leadership,
necessarily affect many people besides themselves.

I recall an incident told me by a friend. He was preparing
to leave for a week-end at St. Martin's House, in Bernards-
ville, New Jersey. His young son overheard his allusion to it
as making a Retreat. "Retreat, Dad!" the boy exclaimed gaily.
"Who's after you, Indians?"

The boy's inquiry was more to the point than he knew. It
is not only *who* is after us, it is *what*. Our complex society is
pursued by accentuated materialism; we must struggle to

maintain and enlarge our spiritual capacities, to calm our nerves to cope with the pressures and tensions that surround us. Some among the world religions long have cherished the spiritual therapy and restorative powers of the Retreat. In comparatively recent years men outside of organized religion—laymen in business and the professions—have recognized more and more that nothing is so creatively helpful, in quite the same way, as getting away from the daily round for an interval of quiet detachment, where they can be silent, think and pray in the Presence of God.

The idea of the Retreat is far from new. How often Jesus made use of it. "And it came to pass . . . that he went out into a mountain to pray, and continued all night in prayer to God." St. Augustine and Francis of Assisi left their abodes to become "grounded in the Love of God." George Fox recounts on the first page of his journal, "I walked abroad in solitary places many days, and often took my Bible and sat in hollow trees and lonesome places till night came on." During one of his Retreats he made his great discovery, "There is one, even Christ Jesus, who can speak to thy condition."

Wars and their aftermath ever leave people "bankrupt inwardly." As Gilbert Kilpack has said, this constitutes an even greater need for us through occasional Retreats "to let the Spirit of God find its peculiar incarnations in our century—this is our great adventure." He has said further, "The first precept of Retreat is that God is never far from any one of us. At rare moments we are all of us aware of this power or beauty, but the thievish disposition of modern secular society steals away our days and years in the very presence of our best intentions. So we should say to ourselves, 'Here, now, is this little speck of time in all eternity; I am going to put everything aside except the Faith that God is the good end of life for me.'

"The second precept of Retreat is simply that we are terribly dependent upon the great heritage of our spiritual forebears, and upon the comradeship of our contemporaries . . . Retreat is a time to lay aside thoughts of business and personal cares, not because they do not have rightful claim on us, but because we habitually permit them to monopolize us, and they must at times be laid aside deliberately if we are to bring to light our spiritually true selves. Retreat is an opportunity to lay aside our argumentative and reasoning mind, and become lowly seekers. It is a time for worship, and for the study of the ways and laws of spiritual discipline."

I feel I am very much the seeker; for that reason I am interested in knowing the experiences and thinking of others on prayer. Though there never was a time when I did not believe firmly in the church or attend its services, I had to learn the extent to which the stubborn self-will which, with its pride and complacency, too often controls us, will not be overcome, neither will the serenity which God is able to give us be forthcoming without a more persistent, intelligent effort on our part to come into and abide in His Presence. I am satisfied that there is only one way for us to find this growth, and that is to learn to pray. To my mind *to learn* is of key importance.

I would like to share with the reader some expressions of thought on the subject which have helped and inspired my own thinking.

In the light of what some people like to think are irreconcilable differences between science and religion, I have been lastingly impressed by a remarkable essay on "Prayer" by the great French-born surgeon and experimental biologist, the late Dr. Alexis Carrel, and should like to include certain excerpts from it here.

"To us men of the West," he said in one place in the essay, "reason seems very superior to intuition. We much prefer intelligence to feeling. Science shines out, while religion is flickering. We seek first of all to develop intelligence in ourselves. As to the non-intellectual activities of the spirit, such as the moral sense, the sense of beauty, *and above all the sense of the holy*, they are almost completely neglected. The atrophy of these fundamental activities makes of the modern man a being spiritually blind. Such an infirmity does not permit him to be an element of good for the constitution of society." Dr. Carrel proceeded to the conclusion, however, that "The fact is, the spiritual shows itself just as indispensible to the success of life as the intellectual and material."

This is comparatively easy to accept as a fact. It is not, however, easy to translate into practice. Some reasoning as to why this is so came in a most interesting letter on the subject of Prayer, from a Trappist monk, to the Laymen's Movement:

". . . We Americans," he suggested, "want everything in a hurry. Yet an interior life dedicated to the practice of prayer is not the work of a year or even ten. We of the high-strung western world seek the natural outlet of nervous energy in action. It takes us a long time to discover the fact that mental activity can become the best and most satisfying kind of action, that is the inter-action which takes place between God and the Praying soul.

"There are two main pitfalls on the road to mastery of the art of prayer. If a person gets what he asks for, his humility is in danger. If he fails to get what he asks for, he is apt to lose confidence. Indeed, no matter whether prayer seems to be succeeding or failing, humility and confidence are two virtues which are absolutely essential."

To my mind "getting what we ask for," and "failing to get what we ask for," put a finger on a crucial aspect of the approach to praying. Is prayer "to get," or it is "to get understanding"? Is it perhaps a little shabby of us to judge God's answers to prayer merely in terms of whether He sends what we ask for—and how soon? Can we afford to forget the need to conform our prayers to our actions? "To pray humbly on rising, and then to behave the rest of the day like a pagan" is both absurd and paraphrases many reminders in the Scriptures as to the spirit and purpose of prayer. None of us want to be guilty of it. The very practical and wise alternative has been suggested: "Very brief thoughts, mental invocations can hold one in the presence of God, then all conduct is inspired by prayer. Prayer, when so understood, becomes a way of life."

This would not deny the value of a set time for prayer. Some urge the value also of a specific place, though I am inclined to think that one of the profoundest blessings of the privilege of prayer is that it is limited by neither time nor place; there is access to God just as readily on the street on the way to a business appointment as in church or kneeling by one's bed before going to the night's rest. However often I turn to the Source for guidance during the business day, one special period I find particularly helpful is the fifteen to thirty minutes of each day, just before retiring, spent in reading and prayer, so much so that a day would be out of joint which went by without it. In this way my final thoughts before going to sleep are centered on Christ, on God, on the spiritual needs of myself and others. I should like to make the point that such a plan may not at all work for you, the reader. There is nothing wrong with everyone coming to this matter in his or her own way. The point is, human nature being frail as it is in the spiritual sense, I sincerely believe all of us need some actual plan; as we grow, it will be adjusted to meet our changing spiritual needs. We can know confidently that "Every technique of prayer is good which draws man nearer to God."

One element which I have found very powerful in the practice of prayer is silence, nor do I think this contradicts what I have said about access to God in prayer even when in the midst of crowds on the street.

To make as effective use of silence as our Quaker friends do is perhaps a little beyond many of us. Yet to learn to be *alone with God* even in the presence of others is a facility which will, I am convinced, bring many benefits if we learn it. There are innumerable times in the course of a day when our thoughts can turn from business or other affairs even for a moment, to be centered on God's Goodness, Christ's love, the needs of our fellowmen.

There is one element in the practice of prayer which some feel hesitant about admitting—in the case of men doubtless for the reason that it is regarded more as a feminine characteristic—and that is *love*. Yet those who write with authority on the subject of prayer almost invariably point out that, if love can be aroused in the hearts of men, no time will be needed to convince them that they must pray, for one will lead naturally to the other.

We will not be reluctant on this point, I think, if we approach it in terms of our privilege in loving God, and remind ourselves that a full understanding of life is impossible without love for God.

As for loving our fellowman, superficially we have been conditioned against it in that by custom love is reserved for the few members of our immediate family. But must we not remind ourselves that such is less than what Christ taught? A man will not carry his share of responsibility for sustaining a brotherhood of men if he does not at the same time love God; neither can he love God if he does not have real love of his fellowman.

We can start with good will, practicing it toward everyone around us. It is good discipline to direct positive good will toward even the most unattractive or improbable person we know. Besides, who knows how it may turn out! Alchemy well may bring out qualities and points of common interest we never suspected.

From the exercises of good will we can move into a positive concern for the well-being of others, and finally to a creative love of men, good or bad, because we have a common Father from Whom we know that man can live together as brothers. In fact, there are signs on all sides that it is becoming progressively difficult to live on any other basis!

As a layman, I believe laymen have a privileged obligation to the church. Rich is our spiritual heritage, and we all owe more than we can repay in our span of life to the church, for preserving Christ's teachings, holding together the body of believers, providing a place for religious instruction for ourselves and our children, and giving spiritual leadership in our home communities, in our nation and to some extent to the whole world. It is the layman's great opportunity, to give himself, his talents, experience and support to the church. In turn the church has to offer an ever-growing opportunity for spiritual growth of the layman, through helping him to see the privileges of bridging the gap between the practical and the spiritual, counseling too as he proceeds with the day-by-day steps which can spiritualize all his daily contacts and, through him, those of his fellowmen.

This plan of life calls for discipline, diligence and persistence. I am convinced that it is being more and more implemented, not only through the convictions of individuals, but the mounting number of prayer circles and such service-offering devices as Dial-a-Prayer and other developments of the kind.

In this connection I think of our individual responsibility in the matter of intercessory prayer. We are often reminded that prayer for others is more effective than prayer for ourselves. If this is so, perhaps it is because in our prayer for others there is less of self. Certainly there is no more sacred trust than intercessory prayer, no place where subtle powers are more likely to assert themselves. It is easy to pray for ourselves, for what we want; to pray for the needs of others requires our *caring*; we cannot redeem His caring for us, unless and until we care for others.

I have no illusions about the power of mere words to persuade people to change their thinking. What I have said here about prayer has been purely personal, and my best hope for it would be that it might help the *chain* of faith and tolerance. Every once in a while a wave of "chain letters" springs up and spreads across the country or even crosses borders of continents. What can come of multiple chains of prayer among peoples is incalculable, if they carry the light of faith, humility and right attitudes.

It goes without saying that it is useless to say "I love all men as my brothers" if, in the recesses of our hearts we dislike and fear so much as one of them. We do *not* love our brothers if we say "I love all men—that is, the ones who believe as I do." We do not love our brothers if we think, "I love all men—except, of course, that one, who is an evil man."

I have been in a perhaps unique position, because of the fact that the Golden Rule was made the cornerstone of our business, to know intimately that it is hard to be patient with people who are ruthless, greedy, selfish, unkind, cruel. In other words, it requires constant vigilance to overcome our human tendency to disapprove, suspect, and dislike people or trends which we cannot understand, hence do not agree with.

If we cannot enter the company of the great prophets, teachers and saints who were great because they achieved an all-embracing compassion, it is nevertheless something for which to strive. We can—and I rather think best through prayer—at least have faith in our fellowman. That, in itself, may help to call forth his best impulses. I know this to be true; in the ordinary round of my business, I have seen it work thousands of times.

As I was thinking along the above lines, I came across a quotation by Dostoevsky on the subject of prayer, and I should like to share it.

"Be not forgetful of prayer," he wrote. "Every time you pray, if your prayer is sincere, there will be new feeling and new meaning in it, which will give you fresh courage, and you will understand that prayer is an education. . . ."

CHAPTER XIII

The Principles Never Change

On a lengthy train trip, in the dining car I chanced to be shown to a table for two. A big, ruddy, All-American fullback type of man occupied the other place, and we fell into conversation, about current events and some of the problems of the country. He was a businessman, with some strong views on our enterprise system. He mentioned a grandfather who made a good living throughout his business life with his buggy-whip factory, adding, "Nobody from the government came around and told him how many buggy whips he could turn out."

"Why do you smile?" he said; "because buggy whips mostly belong in museums nowadays?"

"Well, it may surprise you," I replied, "but they're not too ancient history to me. In fact, when I first went into business, I carried them in stock in my store in Wyoming; they sold from five cents up."

He stared at me for an instant, as though I were some reincarnation of the past. Then his eye fell on a service button I always wear in my lapel. It bears the letters HCSC. "Don't believe I ever ran across one of those before," he said. "What organization does it stand for?"

I explained that the letters stood for the motto of the Penney Company; Honor, Confidence, Service, Cooperation.

He asked my name and I gave it. "Honor, Confidence, Service, Cooperation," he murmured thoughtfully. "Yes, sir, a fine ideal."

"A fine *practical* ideal, we have found it," I replied.

The train rushed along a grade crossing, the bell was a shrill warning, rising and diminishing. "Well," he said, "there's sure room today for ideals that are practical."

"My ideas for doing business were honed on my father's principles; he was a farmer and old-school Baptist preacher, with convictions about carrying on all one's dealings in accord with spiritual standards."

"It's a good way, all right," said my neighbor. He flushed slightly. "I admit I don't always have the nerve to apply them in my business dealings."

The principles underlying our company, and the company motto brought each other into being, you might say, at about the same time. We designated the principles for a long time as our Original Body of Doctrine. While I wouldn't say they are always easy to apply in business, I think people often have an idea, like this man who sat opposite me, that it requires "nerve," and is harder than actually it is.

These are the components of the Original Body of Doctrine for our company:

To serve the public as nearly as we can to its complete
satisfaction.

To offer the best possible dollar's worth of quality and value.

To strive constantly for a high level of intelligent and helpful service.

To charge a fair profit for what we offer, and not all the
traffic will bear.

To apply this test to everything we do: Does it square with
what is right and just?

Read in the light of their meaning, it will be seen why I
say that the rule-of-thumb practices codified in 1914 but in
use in Kemmerer days, and now referred to as Penney Principles, and the qualities chosen for the company motto "brought
each other into being" for they are indivisible, in spirit.

When stressing principles for thought and action, I like
to emphasize two basic conditions. The first of these is that
ethical principles never change; seen or unseen, today standing like massive mountain peaks hidden by clouds, and tomorrow illumined by brilliant subshine, they are always there,
an eternal, unchanging part of life. So fundamental ethical
principles, such as those for example expressed in the Ten
Commandments, have not changed by a hair's breadth since
the dawn of man's creation. Since they are basic, time and cir-
cumstance have no bearing whatever on them. They stand
like Him who said of Himself, "I am the Lord, I change not."

The second basic condition is that ethical principles are exceedingly hard taskmasters. They demand *all*, countenancing
no compromises. There again they are like the unchanging
and unchangeable God with whom, as the Apostle James said,
"there is no variation or shadow due to change."

Thus that man who, having been spiritually enlightened,

proposes to be guided by ethical principles in his worldly affairs, should know at the outset that it will not be easy, nor can he hold a divided allegiance. He cannot serve two masters.

Not long after Jesus called the Twelve he delivered the discourse which Christendom cherishes as The Sermon on the Mount. As we know, much of it is concerned with principles governing human relations. The climax of His teachings on this subject was reached when He said, "Whatsoever ye would that men should do to you, do ye even so to them; for this is the law and the prophets."

Of this simple, beautiful, yet awesome precept, long known as The Golden Rule, Martin Luther said, "All the teachings of these chapters He here ties up in a little bit of a bundle, that everyone may carry it in his bosom, and certainly it is a fine thing that Christ sets before us, precisely ourselves, for an example. Man, thyself, art the master, doctor, and preacher."

Legitimately and honestly applied, it serves all social, family, commercial, political, national and international problems. To obey it completely, in spirit as well as deed, would usher in the Golden Age indeed, and transform the tragedy-ridden world into a garden of peace, plenty, and harmony.

From my father I learned that the great principles we have inherited from the world's experience are not mere statements, to be read occasionally, but *actual forces to be directed upon whatever we do*. Men are, despite much contrary behavior, created in the image and likeness of the living God. This creates at once an obligation and a privilege. As a consequence of my family inheritances and upbringing, into the framework of ideas and ideals which would ultimately be *Me* went the principle, among others, that as I would wish to be done by, so must I do. I was therefore conditioned to regard the Golden Rule as familiar and appealing, when I encountered it under that name.

When I went to work in Longmont, Colorado, for T. M. Callahan and Company, I went to work for proprietors who knew how to organize and conduct a store. The most interesting thing about it, and from my standpoint the most far-reaching, was the advertising of it as a Golden Rule Store and scrupulously operating it that way. It followed that, in the store, I saw demonstrated daily what my father had always taught me. My ideals and a great principle were harnessed together. Without my knowing it, the Golden Rule had lain deep in my soul for many years; now that there were both opportunity and incentive to practice it with every customer I served, I experienced a mounting satisfaction, for every day the fact that it really worked was impressed upon me more and more.

After three years of training with Mr. Callahan, and his partner Guy Johnson, I was offered the third partnership interest in the new store to be opened in Kemmerer. Up to then I had been a student, an observer and, as far as I was able, a practitioner of the Golden Rule as applied by my principals; it was their business, not mine. Now, at Kemmerer, the situation was altogether different. I was fully committed and publicly advertised as an advocate of the Golden Rule. My mind was fully made up to make good on that principle. Just as my father had led me to see, back home in Hamilton, that I must treat neighbors with consideration, so now I was in a position to show consideration for my Kemmerer "neighbors" or customers.

Having been made a partner and put in business for myself, I was lifted to a high level of ambition and lofty outlook.

The responsibility they placed on me and the future their confidence and trust opened up, developed me as nothing else could. It gave me a glimpse of the possibilities inherent in affording men the opportunity likewise for the fullest development of their native talents and capacities. I believed at the time that this was, in the truest sense, "putting the Golden Rule to work." I still believe it. In practice, it was simply a matter of giving men an opportunity to share in the growth and development of the business into which they put their daily work.

Although the partnership plan for expanding to a chain of stores was unique, without precedent in merchandising history, time proved it sound. The largest element in it was the fundamental fact that the most valuable, most durable asset any company can have is *men*. At first I had to proceed slowly because I personally selected every man. I had very definite ideas of the kind of men I wanted. As I saw it, I had no more right to introduce inferior persons into the business than I had to place damaged goods on the shelves.

The time came when I resigned as President of the Company, to put all my time and energy into finding and training our future executives. We opened an office in St. Louis; within four months we received approximately five thousand applications and out of that number accepted sixty-three.

In the early days our "training program" was a rather homespun affair of store meetings after hours, for discussion of subjects relating to the business. Ultimately we developed a training manual, and an Educational Department. The object of all this? Not first and last to make money, but rather to expand and promote the training of men. We knew that if we accomplished this, profits would take care of themselves.

Two convictions shaped the training policy of our Company. I identify them because they are not copyrighted and I believe that they can be made beneficial wherever they are implemented.

The first is that no person should be employed and left as his company found him. One of the greatest instruments an associate (we do not call people employees, for that implies that we give orders which they merely carry out) can have is a forward-looking, hopeful outlook. This was born of the discovery of the crucial fact that it is manifestly impossible to secure better service and more and more business from what may be called dead level ability on the part of a fixed, unchanging person. We have wanted every man and woman who came with us to change, and have given much time and thought to ways and means of bringing that about. Therefore our training has been designed to increase self-respect, deepen self-confidence, multiply efficiency and prepare the individual for that wider responsibility which broadens and enriches lives.

The second conviction is that *no matter what his position or experience in life may be, every person possesses more latent than developed ability, and far more unused power than he is using.* To my mind one of the real opportunities of all businessmen is to develop the latent ability of associates, and unleash the reservoirs of unused power. No business executive or company which succeeds in doing that will fail to profit. Moreover, the person whose powers are thus brought out will profit even more.

This, we believe, is a practical demonstration of the Golden Rule in action in business. Many businessmen and executives have agreed with us, and the number is growing. More and more, men of broad vision and sensitive spirit are coming to believe that the most important element in business is human relations, and that the principal factor in those relations is the spiritual one. This leads many of us to hope prayerfully that the day has dawned when a business institution is not regarded primarily in terms of cash registers, inventories and profits, but as a group of men and women joined by a mutual bond of interest, all working harmoniously toward a common goal—the conservation of human welfare.

Although, being a merchant, I have been speaking of the Golden Rule as applied to the people behind the counter, I should like to mention it briefly in relation to people on the other side of the counter, the customers. We have always believed that business never has been and never will be anything but *serving people,* the public. Yet we like to think of our customers as our neighbors whom it is our privilege to assist in the buying of what they want and need, at the lowest possible prices. In so doing we always strive to respect their rights and wishes. In pursuing this policy of saving money for our customers we effect economies in operation, goods are guaranteed as represented, worthless merchandise is never stocked, and a homelike atmosphere is created within our stores. From what I say you will readily understand that we believe the Golden Rule is essentially *The Rule of Service.* My experience has been that people are always responsive to any attempt to render them a genuine service. The principle of service is the same, no matter whether it is applied in business, industry, domestic, national or international affairs. The plight of most of our world today calls for a finer and deeper sense of service than has ever been known. American business and businessmen must do no less than their best in lightening the burdens and brightening the shadows under which mankind labors today.

In the broad field of employer-employee relations, two things tend to stand in the way of applying the Golden Rule inclusively. The first, and perhaps the most difficult, is age-old customs and habits of thought. Among these is class antagonism, too slowly being allayed by better understanding and mutual appreciation; this breeds distrust and suspicion which, where they do not rule out cooperation altogether, make it extremely difficult. It is a benefit to no one and constitutes a real liability to our democratic way of life and the free enterprise that is one of that way's traditional expressions. The only true conception of business is of a two-way street. The need today is for statesmanlike and prophetic leadership in business principles, distinguished by character, intelligence and capacity "to see life truly and see it whole."

Instead of battling in the dark, all elements of business and industrial life should "fraternize in the light." We all profess to yearn for a state of peace and good will between men. So far as I can see, universal use of the Golden Rule is the only way really to achieve it.

As I have said earlier in this book, I observe great gains in the quality of human relations in business. But I believe we are at a point where we must remind ourselves early and often that, as someone has said, "Fraternity is impossible without piety." That means simply that we cannot set ourselves at rights one with the other, solve our vexing problems, or move out into a new area of national greatness unless we truly enshrine God at the center of things. Oscar L. Joseph has well said, "Our most pressing need therefore is to create a new soul and a new conscience, a new will, under the educating and emancipating influence of new ideals, distinguished by their spiritual emphasis." Nothing is more clearly established in history than that, wherever the Gospel of Christ and Christianity have been honored, a way out of critical circumstances, problems which may have seemed insoluble, and confusions which appeared hopeless, has been found.

Is not this the rallying cry to all of us for the application of the Golden Rule to business and industry? I give it as my profound conviction that no other rule is competent to solve our problems in this area and insure the safety of the future. The Golden Rule is founded upon the primary, natural law that men shall be just in their dealings with one another. The possibility of loving one's neighbor is often debated, but no one questions the necessity to be just to everyone. Harry Emerson Fosdick says in his *Meaning of Service* that the keeping of the Golden Rule is conditioned upon a generous and sympathetic imagination and active good will. He further says, "No one is just who does not put himself in the place of those with whom he deals. And to do that one must see men as he does stained glass in a cathedral window, not from without in, but from within out . . . To do for others what we desire to have done for us is not a negative ideal. Too often justice is pictured in terms of *abstinence from rank injustice.* Not to be cruel, not to oppress the poor or to grind the faces of the needy, that is to be just. But the Golden Rule *cannot be negatively kept.* Justice is positive. It means the painstaking bestowal upon other lives of the same sort of constant, sacrificial ministry by which we ourselves have lived and without which we could not really live at all."

Along with the Law of Justice, the Golden Rule is also, to

my mind, the Law of Love. Instead of being regarded as a beautiful yet unattainable ideal—as unfortunately many do regard it even today—this is an extremely practical Rule for the everyday lives of men and women. "Thou shalt love thy neighbor as thyself," wrote Moses in the Book of Leviticus. The Psalmist, out of the wealth of vast experience, touched upon this vital matter when he said, "Behold, how good and how pleasant it is for brethren to dwell together in unity! It is like the precious ointment upon the head, that ran down upon the beard, even Aaron's beard; that went down to the skirts of his garments; as the dew of Hermon, and as the dew that descended upon the mountains of Zion; for there the Lord commanded the blessing, even life forever more."

On the lips of Jesus the Golden Rule and the Law of Love were perfectly joined when He said, "This is my commandment, that ye love one another, as I have loved you. Greater love hath no man than this, that a man lay down his life for his friends."

When I draw on my experiences with practice of the Golden Rule in business the emphasis in my own mind is on the word *practice*. I think it requires *practice*, like any art or skill.

Though I do earnestly suggest, for the reader's thoughtful reflection, the idea that the person who gives less than the application of fundamental Christian principles to his daily occupation and relationships is missing his opportunity, toward that occupation, toward his country, and for himself, I would not imply for a moment that my own practices are all perfected. It seems to me one of the great reassurances of living that we can never come to the end of our right to try harder to improve, and to keep on trying. Forms and methods of applying Christian principles will perhaps always differ with people. We can say the same of architecture; it will find many and varying forms of expression, but it will always start with the compass and try-square. In terms of our company the components of our Original Body of Doctrine always have been our compass and try-square: let me recapitulate them:

To serve the public, as nearly as we can, to its complete satisfaction.

To offer the best possible dollar's worth of quality and value.

To strive constantly for a high level of intelligent and helpful service.

To charge a fair profit for what we offer—and not all the traffic will bear.

To apply this test to everything we do: "Does it square with what is just and right?"

So with our store motto. In its elements—Honor, Confidence, Service, Cooperation—it synthesized the guiding principles to which we wished to bear witness in the individual and all-around relationships of our business.

I think I might just interject here, that the main reason for my participation in Rotary, through associations not only in my own country but around the world, is the close resemblance between its approach and ours. Rotary action must square with these ideals:

Is it the truth?

Is it fair to all concerned?

Will it build good will and better friendships?

Will it be beneficial to all concerned?

It is self-evident that both these sets of objectives derive from the Golden Rule. Any number of analogies to Golden

Rule practice can be found. I happen to be fond of one between the opportunity it offers to the individual, and one of my father's uses for the Barlow 2-bladed knife which he always carried with him, and which I now carry as a daily reminder. On his farm, whenever he came across so much as a single small weed, the kind other men might not even notice or, seeing, would pass by, he cut it out with this knife. The action bespoke his pride in keeping his pastures clean; but I see Golden Rule symbolism in it too. Eliminating harmful elements in the form of weeds, it marked a careful clearing away of discord, opening up to the main growth a freer flow of light and air.

Another analogy occurs to me, calling back to mind a homespun but, to me, telling observation once made by an uncle of mine. It seems that a young relative was making rather hard work of familiarizing himself with a habit of a certain character-building type. My uncle understood, and sympathized. "Let him be," he advised. "He's got to breathe it through his own nose."

Golden Rule practice is a bit like that. We'll be able to practice it when we breathe it through our own nose.

VIEW FROM THE NINTH DECADE

CHAPTER XIV

"We Do Not Bathe in the Same River Twice . . ."

There is a Hindu saying, "We never bathe in the same river twice." Many meanings can be read into it; its thought either occurs or is suggested in sayings of many peoples. I thought of this recently while walking part of the distance to my office. It is an old cliché that nothing can be done about the weather. Meteorologically it would seem true, with the possible exception of the system of seeding clouds.

But I am thinking more particularly of a climate which we can create around us, for good or ill, by what I would call *starting out right* at the beginning of the day. We have all had experience with the kind of person who is not at his best, let us say, at the start of the working day. Years ago Fontaine Fox, the cartoonist, immortalized the type in one of his newspaper cartoon features built around the troubles of a character named The Terrible Tempered Mr. Bang, a man to whom it was generally unwise to speak first, particularly in the morning before he had collected himself for the day's demands.

In a measure, I think, we can individually create a "portable climate," as it were, which can help to counteract pressures and surface hostilities amid the complex tensions produced by our living pace. I must admit I have not always done as I would wish or should have and there is little excuse for back-sliding because from the beginnings of our business the spontaneous friendly interest was a key to the spirit of our dealings with the public.

What currents of good feeling are released when we take care to *start out right*, by which I mean, to practice from the waking moments of the day, creative pleasantness. I am not thinking of garrulity; I believe the simple friendly word or two has a very long reach.

Wonderful moments have come to me as a result of small ventures in getting through a melancholy shell to a person I felt was right there behind it all the time. The late Charles Steinmetz, the American electrical engineering genius, was wont to describe scientific discoveries as "the rewards of curiosity." In the course of my business career, curiosity as to whether I could get through resistances to the real person has brought me many rewards. I remember one instance in particular.

Commuting for many weeks to my work in the city, at the Grand Central Station I went underground to catch the shuttle across to Times Square, thence to a subway train to 34th Street. My attention was caught by a free-lance porter who, because he was not part of the Red Cap contingent which had the concession in the station, was obliged to pick up what business he could at the subway stairs and other fringe areas. I think what attracted me to him was that he never seemed very hopeful that he would pick up business. He had a sad and anxious expression, his shoulders drooped, his eyes seemed perpetually dull with resignation.

One day I said, "Good morning. I believe it's going to be a fine day." He shot me a startled, sidelong look; I saw his lips move slightly, though only a faint wordless sound came forth.

I began looking for him each morning. In one way I dreaded seeing him because it would mean he wasn't being kept busy. Each morning I spoke some small word of greeting. There could be any number of reasons for his unresponsiveness: some heavy burden might be weighing down his mind; he might be an inherently shy man, who found communication difficult. I don't know how long it was before I noticed the first faint quickening of the eye when he saw me coming toward him.

One morning his lips moved and I caught the words, " 'Morning, sir." At that instant a big, red-faced man rushed up, thrust a heavy suitcase at him, exclaimed peremptorily, "Here—come along——"

It went along quite a while on that brief exchange. I would bid him good morning and make some little remark; he would reply, " 'Morning, sir." But I felt blessed by the small smile which in time accompanied the brief words. It grew into one of those almost invisible vignettes—almost, but not quite—to be looked forward to. From time to time during the day, answering my mail or holding business conferences, I would think of it gratefully. Into his slight smile each morning I read that he too was getting some feeling of friendliness, warmth.

At one period, when my business days were crowded with unusually heavy responsibilities, the only time I had for any exercise was early in the morning, and I rode horseback in Central Park.

None of these incidents I recall are of particular interest in themselves, but they help me to make a point which I have found from experience has its uses.

One morning I came alongside another rider on the bridle path. My attention was caught by his posture astride the horse, a rather high-spirited and uncommonly beautiful roan mare which he sat loosely, his whole body curved in such an inertia of indifference that it seemed that he would surely be thrown if his mount should shy suddenly.

There had been a sky full of ragged, scudding high overcast. It had rained in the night, the bridle path was slick and muddy. But the sky was lightening, with a prospect of the sun breaking through quite soon.

"Good morning," I said, reining up. "Nice morning."

"Don't know where you get that," he grumbled. "Mud—look at the mud!" He was looking down, but I was looking up.

"From the look of that patch of blue up there, I'd say the sun will be out in about four minutes." His reply was a sort of grunt. He ticked his mount's flank with his heel; as they splashed off, I couldn't help thinking that he'd gone to a lot of bother to come out to ride if he was going to get as little out of it as all that.

One never cares to assume the role of Pollyanna, but I tell myself often, taking care to start out right can have side-effects that are creative. There are a thousand ways of starting out right on the day. Undoubtedly some of them will never be missed if we don't exercise them; yet who is to say

that one of them may not affect some human being in a
way that will remain beneficial for years? Do we not many
times become our own enemies, by withholding that word
or two we could have spoken, the little gesture of notice we
might have made, often perhaps to the person who was not
expecting to be noticed, and who would therefore be the more
pleased and possibly helped?

I recall a period in which I was certainly my own worst
enemy in this respect. Harboring hostility and bitterness toward a banking institution, which I told myself should have
behaved differently toward me in a critical business situation,
pettishly I made it my practice, when walking daily to my
office, always to walk on the far side of the street, in order
to avoid passing the bank's main entrance and its doorman.

One morning it suddenly came to me that the action was
not only silly and destructive in itself, but that I was ad-
versely coloring my whole day with such an attitude. Even
if my bitterness were well-founded—and it was not, although
it took some years to bring myself around to seeing that—it
made something less than an intelligent picture, for me to be
trying to take it out on the doorman (even though I hope and
believe he was never aware of it).

I took myself in hand. One day, coming up with the doorman, I said, "Good morning; lovely day, isn't it?"

"Sure it is that, sir," said he in the great booming voice
of a man content to take life as he finds it. "A fine day for
a good walk it is, sir. I guess you enjoy a walk. I often see you
passing down the other side of the street, there, yes sir."

"I just thought it was time to change sides," I said.

Certainly I have no wish to pat myself on the back for
coming to my senses; I should have done so much sooner. In

any case, thereafter my regular morning walk to the office was pleasant in a way I had not before known.

In the scale of things that trouble people and the world, these experiences on the face of them seem small and unimportant. Yet I am not so sure. I don't believe we have scratched the surface of the power lying in *little things* to raise the harmony of living. Starting the day right is like cash-and-carry shopping, requiring no expensive overhead. It has been the means of my learning little things about human nature, and living, which I wouldn't have missed for the world.

Not long ago I was riding downtown in a bus. I got an impression that the majority of the passengers had, as we used to say, got up on the wrong side of the bed. The driver stood the brunt of absurd questions, quarrelsome demands that he change five-dollar bills and all the rest of it, with what we describe as the patience of Job. It happens that I am particularly devoted to the Book of Job, because of his sufferings and because he was tempted by the devil and resisted.

By the time we reached my stop, harassment of the driver had fallen off somewhat. As the bus slowed down I said to him, "I think you must be a Christian." He looked startled, and I added, "Your patience has been pretty sorely tried this morning. You'd almost have to be a Christian to handle it."

"Well," he said with a broad smile, "I try to be." Before he closed the door he called after me, "Now good morning to you, sir!"

Little things, yes. But I wonder whether it isn't more little things than big that make the world go round.

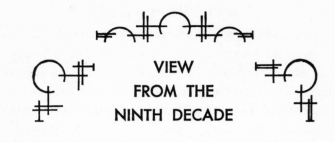

**VIEW
FROM THE
NINTH DECADE**

CHAPTER XV

Crisis Is Constant, Only the Forms Change

I have noted how often politicians, ministers and other public figures emphasize that the days we are living in are a time of crisis and grave danger. The implication usually is that this is news. It is not news, if I may say so. I would question, rather, when has mankind's day *not* been a time of crisis and grave danger? We are in perpetual and everlasting flux; we are always under crisis which differs only in variety.

Though the only new thing about our times is the forms of crises, obviously our period is one of manifold problems and must be reckoned with as such. It is also not news that there are no easy solutions, no identical precedents to go by. Since our way of life will never outdistance crises—a good thing, for it presents us with the incentives of progress—nor will it automatically continue to function, what then do we have, upon which to rely for inspiration and guidance?

My mind turns to the composite strengths which produced

the country, and on which our forefathers confidently relied. I read again the words of our Declaration of Independence, in which our ideals were originally stated, and am impressed with their timeless freshness, for that is a mark of universal truth. Its author, Thomas Jefferson, crystallized in ringing words and phrases, ideas that were clearly God-inspired. I have an idea that all of us could well make a habit of re-reading the Declaration of Independence at least once a year. It has had a part in shaping the history of the world, and the more we study and understand it, the more it lights our understanding of the unique character of this country of ours.

Let no one give you the impression that re-reading this document is a colorless undertaking; it is a thrilling experience which I recommend.

On one occasion Jefferson wrote, "I know that laws and institutions must go hand in hand with the progress of the human mind. As that becomes more developed, more enlightened; as new discoveries are made, new truths disclosed, institutions must advance also, and keep pace with the times. We might as well require a man to wear, still, the coat which fitted him as a boy, as to have civilized society remain ever under the regimen of barbarous ancestors."

Now it seems to me that Jefferson's words have an exact application to the world of today, where barbarous oppression and ruthless control of millions of human lives still exist. Here, nearly two centuries ago, we demanded and fought for our freedoms. Today the God-given boons we have so long enjoyed are still denied to millions of our brothers in other lands. Do we—you and I—really recognize what this means to us? Are we correspondingly grateful for the place in the sun which is available to every American? Do we comprehend our opportunities to develop and use our individual talents, appreciating those opportunities?

Above all, do we grasp the grave responsibility which goes along with all this?

In this connection Jefferson also said: "The station which we occupy among the nations of the earth is honorable, but awful. Trusted with the destinies of this Republic, the only monument of human rights and the sole depository of the sacred fire of freedom, from hence it is to be lighted up in other regions of the earth, *if other regions of the earth ever become susceptible to its benign influence.* And to what sacrifices ought not these considerations animate us? To what compromises of opinion and inclination, to maintain harmony and union among ourselves, and to preserve from all dangers this hallowed ark of human hope and human happiness."

It is as though this great man saw across the centuries our present position of leadership in spreading our gospel of men's freedom to all the world.

It is regrettable that the clear vision and courage with which men like Jefferson enunciated our American Ideals is too rarely encountered today. Perhaps the problems of adjustment to the international situation are too great, too difficult to define and cope with. Perhaps we, as a people, have absorbed a sort of despairing feeling that there is no simple answer to these complex problems.

I make bold to own to a deep conviction that, on the contrary, there *is*, for I am a simple man with a single-minded approach to life. I would remind the reader that the problems faced by the men who founded this country were, in their way, no less complex than ours today. We were then a *little* country, our resources were hard-won and small. We had no power in international affairs. In short, we had nothing material or tangible with which to establish our place with the great powers of the world. Nothing, in fact, *except God, and His Power*. The only real force with which we faced our early problems was a *spiritual* force. It was the reason why we succeeded. Despite any and all appearances, there has never been, there never will be, any earthly power that can equal the irresistible force of spiritual ideals.

Does this sound like a horse-and-buggy concept for this modern world? I would not have the reader think that I would turn the clock back to our early days of deprivation and primitive living. I would not have us relinquish the comforts and luxuries we enjoy today. We have come a long way from our Spartan years, earning the fruits of our labor and ingenuity.

I would, however, have us—*all of us*—turn back our thinking and our attitudes to those which breathed life and glory into this country. I would have us realize, *every day*, the limitless blessings conferred upon us through our American ideals. I would ask the reader to remember—*every day*—that the blessings we enjoy come to us from the Giver of all gifts, God, through His guidance of powers received at His hand.

I have stated that I am a simple man, with a single-minded approach to life. I believe wholeheartedly that, without God in our hearts, we have nothing, and can achieve nothing of true value.

With God, we are everything. I have every confidence in our ability, with God, to keep our leadership in world affairs.

I am not overly impressed, and I am certainly not frightened, by the scientific advances represented by sputniks, missiles and other new forms for destruction. I am not even frightened by the preliminary photographs of the other side of the moon. I would, on the other hand, be frightened to think that we might lose our spiritual motivations, in our competition with the achievements of other governments. We still have far to go to achieve peace and serenity in the hearts of men. Realization of this goal should dominate all of our endeavors. It is inevitable that we would see a threat in the arrogance of those seeking control by material means of men's minds and the forces of nature. Those who imagine they can usurp God's prerogatives and power are asking outright for His wrath; they are sowing the seeds of their own destruction. I do not mean for an instant to say that we should, or can, simply fold our hands in the face of this, and wait. By no means! I do mean that our very salvation depends, as indeed it always has, on our recognition of and reliance on Divine Power for our guidance.

What I say here will not influence directly any of the decisions taken by men, those who, to a degree, hold our lives and our future in their hands. Yet, if I make myself clear to *you,* the reader, your influence will spread out and wield power to overcome errors of thought and action. Each, by realizing *and using* Divine Power, can be a strand in an irresistible cable of force for good that can reach and bless the farthest parts of this earth.

We often hear people say, with resignation, "But I am only one person, one mind, one pair of hands. What can *I* do?" Do not give that thought house-room. Jesus Christ was "only one person" on this earth—and we shall never see the end of His influence and power. The part assigned to us is to *deny* despair and helplessness in the face of what is happening in the world. It is also to act responsibly, with decision and with courage, for the restoration of values which were passed on to us by the men who originally gave us our American Ideals. Our job is to man the barricades against those false runners bearing the specious gospel of expediency, neither accepting nor permitting actions and decisions which our conscience and faith deny are true and right.

The standards of our founding fathers were ethical standards and when called upon they sacrificed life itself for them. They made no distinction between personal and public ethics. Men did not do in public situations what, if done as individuals, would see them jailed. What was right for an individual to do applied to acts of government as well.

It often appears today that, as a nation, we overlook the validity and creative value of these ideals. On every hand we observe departures from strict honesty and condone them. The white of right and the black of wrong are too often blurred into a confused gray. With deplorable cynicism we have come to accept legal tricks, used to circumvent laws made for legitimate purposes.

Perhaps we are allowing the whole fabric of our life to become too cluttered and complicated. Perhaps we have lost our simplicity, that straightforward, uncompromising honesty which was built-in among the men who formulated our code of American Ideals. Recently I read this description of an important businessman: "an old-fashioned free-enterpriser, creative, independent, dogged in purpose." If I could describe a constructive goal for young people starting out to make their way in the world, I could hardly do better than this. If we have, indeed, lost our simplicity, our only hope of regaining it rests with every individual who learns to think, honestly and independently. If Americans, as a whole and as individuals, any longer delay returning and living up to those ideals we shall not only be failing our tradition and inheritances, but all mankind as well. This is a sobering thought, one which might well guide us daily, in our least as well as greater decisions and actions. I am disturbed when I reflect how many of our original American Ideals have fallen away from simplicity and truth, becoming mere clichés, familiar stereotypes that have lost their meaning for many of us.

If I may be allowed to cite a common denominator between our American Ideals, and the founding principles of our company, it is their inherent simplicity; they are timeless and will always work, if we make it so. I like to think of this as an incentive to young people in preparing themselves against periodic attitudes of cynicism. It seems to me there is a rather simple formula (note I do not say an easy one), namely, "Respect yourself, respect others, work hard and continuously at some worthwhile thing." The formula served me well in early, difficult days, and I have seen thousands of young people get ahead who used it as their rule.

When we use words such as liberty, freedom, the rights of people, individual initiative, must we not, at the same time, think what the words *meant*, when they were first used to establish our country under God's laws? If we don't think, isn't it rather like *repeating* the Lord's Prayer, with no meditation on its *inward* meaning? *

It is a strange thing that perhaps we sometimes overlook the analogy between the so-called "self-made man" who, in

* The foregoing thoughts, among others, were expressed at Baylor University's *Seventh Conference on American Ideals* (November 20 and 21, 1959). The purpose of this Conference is to reevaluate the American Way of Life, and to reaffirm the American principles of freedom and democracy.

typical Horatio Alger fashion, made his way up from nothing or at least very little in the way of material advantages, and this nation which, without blueprint or precedent, built a structure some had dreamed about, but the like of which none had ever seen. No other nation in modern history began with so little and accumulated so much. Relying upon God and His teachings, and nothing else and no one except themselves, our forebears tamed a vast wilderness and made the desert to "rejoice, and blossom as the rose." They created a new system of government based on the fundamental principle of man's endowment by his Creator with life, liberty and certain inalienable rights and, on this foundation hewed out the mightiest, most productive and strongest industrial system the world ever saw. Along with it, they devised a new economic system on the eminently just underlying principle that "the laborer is worthy of his hire."

We ask ourselves often, how and why did these things happen here, and nowhere else in the world. There must be a reason.

My idea of the reason would be that we are a people with an extraordinary capacity for faith. That seems to me the only way we can account for the remarkable things that have happened here.

From the things accomplished in the span since our history as a country began, we can draw certain conclusions about the nature of this faith.

It has always been dynamic, never abstract nor static. It has been an irresistible incentive to creative, constructive effort, never soporific, conducive to inertia. It has bred optimism and hope, endowing us with a provocative vision of better things to come. This faith has fostered ambition which, in turn, has propagated a healthy aversion to the *status quo*, nourishing an irresistible drive to make them what they ought to be. It nourished at once a lofty idealism and evoked a spirit of devotion to the self-appointed tasks.

A faith that has been able to do all of these things for Americans in the past ought to interest us greatly and I believe that in the main it does. A minority of cynics on the subject is inevitable, but they speak for only themselves. The heart of America has lost none of its soundness, and her people are today as much men and women, and as much young people and children, as were our fathers of old.

What kind of faith inspired, strengthened and led them in those early days? What kind of faith constitutes the bedrock of American thought, hope and life today?

It was, is now, and always will be a religious faith in God as the Creator, Supreme Being and Father of us all.

Any study of the history of America may logically start with the sublime opening of the Book of Genesis: "In the beginning God created the heaven and the earth." In the same order, the founders of this Republic believed, God not only led them to these shores, but guided them also in the origination of the type of society they developed here. With the Scriptures in one hand, and the axe or hoe in the other, they labored without ceasing to lay the foundation on which today we continue to build. What other nation can cite so spiritually-guided an origin?

Our fathers believed implicitly that God is in our world, that man is accountable to Him, and that He will sustain those who put their trust in Him. Faith endowed the Pilgrims' bleak prospect with infinite possibilities; not for a moment did they doubt that the God who had led them across the ocean to raw wilderness would enable them to remain and succeed in those things they aspired to do. Today we live in a turbulent present, and face an inscrutable future, but no more turbulent or inscrutable, proportionately, than our forebears faced. What, therefore, is our primary, most urgent, need? Is it not such a faith in God as theirs? The wisdom of men, alone and unaided, will never sufficiently fortify us for the continuing struggles. If we are unwise enough to put our trust in mere man, we shall certainly reap nothing except failure and disappointment. The forces involved in the global conflict swirling about us are so vast, so complicated, that the mind of man reels before them. It is doubtful that even those who have unleashed them can any longer be sure of controlling them.

Is there any way out for us?

One, I am convinced. First, renewing and strengthening our faith in God and His eternal purposes, we must make it *in practice* the dominant, governing power of our lives, individually and collectively. Second, we must put ourselves in His hands, in whole and humble obedience to His will.

So far as I can see, that is all there is to it.

God did not create this chaos in which we live today; willful and misguided men are responsible for that. But God is waiting to be asked to change them and, if we are receptive to His will, in His own good time and way, He will do so.

I like to remind myself of a question posed by Dr. Norman Vincent Peale as to faith and belief.

> Believe that God is with you, that He will help you if you will let Him. That is one of the greatest truths religion has to offer, and it is one of the simplest. 'I can do all things', as the Bible says, because God provides

the power, the talent, the drive, the guidance. If you actually *believed*, really *felt* that God was going to help you in any task you had to do, would you have a moment's doubt of your ability to do it? Of course not.

He stands ready, right now, to help you. All you need do is ask. . . .*

Relating our need to find solutions for world troubles to faith, if individually and collectively we actually believe and feel that God is going to help us, will we have any doubt of our finding the solutions? "Of course not. All we need do is ask."

It is not only our God-given privilege to find solutions, it is our responsibility. We shall not be true to ourselves, to our ideals or to our historic responsibility if we falter or fail in the face of the world's dire need. What, then, shall we do, in order to condition ourselves for the task that the privilege of leadership calls us to do? It seems to me the answer is clear.

After reaffirming our faith in God, with equal earnestness we should reaffirm our faith in the freedom of man, as enunciated by our forefathers and instilled in our religious, political and economic systems. There are many signs that we have fallen behind somewhat in this. We must make up for lost time.

I could go into evidences of our compromising with freedom, and would, were it not for my strong conviction that we need to concentrate first on correcting our course spiritually. "And ye shall know the truth, and the truth shall make you free."

It is not the point that we are living in one of those critical,

* Copyright by the Hall Syndicate, Inc; 1956.

decisive periods of history. The point is, "Which way shall we take?"

It should not be difficult to decide. In one direction lie freedom, progress and happiness; in the other lie enslavement and its inseparable companion, misery. Those are our alternatives, about which there is no mystery.

Our obligation is clear, to ourselves and to mankind in our times. It is nothing less than a courageous, sincere reaffirmation of the firm, constructive, traditional faith in God and His laws which has made this country great. Greatness carries with it obligations. The least request left us by the founders of our country is that we meet our obligations. Daniel Webster was wont to say, "God grants *liberty* only to those who love it and are ready to guard and defend it." I think we have gone beyond the point in history where we can allow ourselves to think of freedom merely for ourselves. We say, when the subject comes up, that we are concerned about freedom for all peoples. We agree when J. Edgar Hoover says, "The banners of Christ can lead the way to the moral and spiritual rebirth of our great nation," with all that implies of extending the free world. Our houses of worship are multiplying, millions more people are attending the services of worship held in them. We maintain thousands of Sunday Schools, though approximately half of our children of high school age or under still receive no consecutive religious instruction at all. We look askance at divorce statistics though one of the traditional foundation stones of our country is the integrity of the home, yet we do not ask ourselves with any great urgency where the trouble lies, how it shall be overcome.

I was one of the fortunate ones. Worldly goods were nota-

ble chiefly for their absence, but I was taught to honor God's
Holy Law and that He could not be served by less than a
whole heart. There were many homes like mine in my early
days, and there are many of them now. I would be very surprised if any reader were to have the slightest doubt that the
strength, stability, continuity and very life of our nation depends more upon such homes than upon any other single
factor.

What is *each one of us* to do about the hard fact which we
must face today, namely, that just as our fathers fought to
institute the *American way of life*, so must we fight to maintain it.

How? By what way?

Again it seems to me, everything starts with the individual.

Each of us must undertake prayerfully to conform his private life to the will of God. We need to remind ourselves,
that "the fear of the Lord is the beginning of wisdom."

Each of us should want, and see a clear reason for dedicat-
ing ourselves to preserving, and making more vital, those spiritual values—faith, honor, charity, unselfishness, humility,
justice—which built the country's greatness, at the same time
keeping the country materially and militarily strong.

That the impression of the greatness of our country and its
source is not solely our own image is indicated in a comment
by the French politician and writer, Alexis de Tocqueville (in
his four-volume work, *Democracy in America*, which is still
relevant because of the originality of insight and vision with
which it discusses the shortcomings and advantages of the
political and social system, justifying democracy and predict-
ing its ultimate triumph).

"I sought," he says, "for the greatness and genius of

America in her commodious harbors and her ample rivers, and it was not there; in the fertile fields and boundless prairies, and it was not there; in her rich mines and her vast world commerce, and it was not there.

"Not until I went into the churches of America and heard her pulpits aflame with righteousness did I understand the secret of her genius and power. *America is great because she is good,* and if ever America ceases to be good, America will cease to be great. . . ."

Not by any means do I think that, with our sporadic letdown in values and practices, America has ceased to be good. But it seems to me that in De Tocqueville's analysis there is something to bear in mind, and that the responsibility rests on every one of us to see that America does not "cease to be good."

Additionally, each of us as Americans bears the responsibility to exemplify liberty, justice and equality of rights under God *for all men of all time.* America has done this instinctively in the past; she can do it in the future even more convincingly.

In this connection I am reminded of two related thoughts expressed by Calvin Coolidge during a brief meeting I was privileged to have with him when he was in the White House. For several reasons I welcomed the opportunity to meet him. He was the first President of the United States I had ever met. More important even to me, I had the feeling that we looked the same way at some things.

When I went for the appointment I was very conscious that this was a very busy man, and I took the precaution of asking the appointment secretary how I could tell when to leave.

"Oh," he laughed, "he'll tell you—when he sits on the edge of his chair you'll know you should leave." He added that I would probably be there about twenty minutes. Not wanting to stay long enough to be dismissed, when twelve minutes had passed, I started to get up. "Sit still," said Mr. Coolidge, in a voice that reminded me of the dry rustle of leaves in late autumn along one of the creeks back home in Hamilton, "some of your ideas interest me."

In common with most people in the country I knew that the qualities of industry and thrift were very much to his taste, though I had not expected him to speak of them in relation to my business policies and facets of my business career which he evidently knew.

I knew I had not been mistaken about our thinking alike in some things when he remarked, in connecting up a point, "Men grow in people's eyes because of their virtue and character." He added, "We pass a lot of laws to enforce the Ten Commandments, but there is no way of substituting the authority of law for the virtues of men." I have never forgotten these two remarks in particular, and it was interesting to me later that Herbert Hoover, commenting on the memorial in Washington to the late Senator Robert A. Taft, should in a sense amplify Mr. Coolidge's thought by saying, "The thing that matters is that *the memory of those who have stood for moral principles in public life* must be preserved."

In our American structure, the individual is supreme. In that opposing view which is disturbing the prospect of peace in the world, there *is* no individual; only a human mass, dominated, herded. In this picture the individual's only estimated value lies in how much he can produce: how many tons of coal he can mine, how many acres he can sow, how many bricks he can lay. If he does not produce, the penalty is sure and swift; it is as though he never existed. He is not eligible for the privilege of choice; he can do only what he is told.

In the one kind of thinking, then, man is an entity and has an inherent importance, with free choice, free will, and divine dignity as a person. In the other kind, nothing is asked, expected or accepted from him but obedience.

Between the two can be discerned the very nub of our peril. In a free nation, where the individual is of first importance, that importance is nevertheless not free, in that it carries with it a heavy responsibility, a *quid pro quo*. Namely, he must be worthy of the trust, by being a responsible citizen, by dealing reasonably and fairly with his fellow men. The free choices he makes cannot be jungle choices. They must be based on justice—if you will, on the Golden Rule. He must deal with others as he expects to be dealt with by them. Granted that this is stern discipline, but on it depends his very survival as a free human being. So too does the ultimate survival of this country depend on him and his fellow free men. Every man who fails, in even little things, must share responsibility for the loss, to every man, woman and child in the country, of some part of that priceless gift of freedom. No, no one can claim that the American way of life is an easy way, for we must all make a full measure of contribution to it: in hard work to sustain and preserve it, in a responsible attitude toward government because we *are* that government in terms of planning, building, sharing; in short, we must display the attitudes and actions that mark the man of character.

To reiterate a point, to my mind, it all begins with the home and the individual. If we are to keep America safe and secure, it must begin with the American family and its preservation. We must concern ourselves deeply, and with a wise love, about our children. We must know where they are, what they are doing, what they are learning. We must take a hand, day by day, in teaching them, not controlling, but guiding them. Their hands receive the torch from ours.

The family, each family, is a microcosm of the whole country. Thus America is a projection of the family unit. If *it* is sound and right, we need have no fears for America; we need practice only eternal vigilance.

And there, I think, is the job lying at hand for everyone. Not a vague, abstract, remote job, to be elected or rejected at one's own discretion, but a privileged, concrete, practical, day-by-day job, embodying an immense concept of responsibility but offering immense satisfactions, too.

We sometimes regard history and historic influences as far-off and only dimly consequential. On the contrary, do not our inheritances bring the main job into the most positive kind of relation to our times?

We *can* do the job with the help of God. We *can* do it with faith in Him. We *can* do it with prayer.

This is what I believe, and all my experience tells me it is true.

CHAPTER XVI

We Are All Advertisers

As a merchant I have an ever-inquiring mind as to advertising. I have some strong convictions about the principles that govern it, or should. To me there should be no question of its being covered by less than the same code of ethics which distinguishes all sound human relationships.

In a broad sense we are all advertisers, with special emphasis on public relations. We may not be one of those who decide on the spending of hundreds of thousands of dollars for sponsorship of an automobile-account show on TV, or of a Leonard Bernstein conducting performances of the New York Philharmonic Orchestra. Nevertheless, we are advertisers of our individual integrity and standards in terms of the quality of our everyday dealings. Our public relations are the open evidence of our approach to ethics, business morality and the arterial relationships of living.

As a businessman I have a direct interest in the forces of

advertising and public relations as they have to do with selling goods to consumers. What a company believes in and stands for philosophically should be as discernible in its advertising as the sign over its place of business, the open and aboveboard disclosure of the quality to be expected in the goods that it sells. It should be as readily possible to tell the one by looking at the other; no daylight should show between what is professed and what is done. As with individuals, a company which professes one standard and practices another—for expediency, profit, or any other reason—not only injures itself but shares in giving business a bad name. It is very gratifying to me, therefore, to note business as a whole progressing steadily in practice of moral as well as material values, and respect for them as part and parcel of service.

Reduced to its simplest definition, advertising is a message from someone with something to sell, to those he hopes need and will buy it.

What, then, is the first obligation of the advertiser?

To me it is simply stated: to come into the market place, that complex of media comprising newspapers, magazines, radio and TV, with the story of what he has to offer told simply, clearly and honestly. His obligation also is to convey to his hoped-for customers the nature of the business he conducts, what advantages it has to offer those who respond.

Advertising and the element of competition are closely allied. I deplore those advertising methods which seek to make people believe that all goods and services are unworthy except those of the immediate advertiser. In the first place, it could not possibly be true; and even an implication which is untrue is to offer a disservice at the outset; it sows distrust and cynicism and, by suggesting the mean-spirited idea that no advertiser but the one whose goods are being advertised is honest and sincere, it contains the seeds of its own destruction.

I oppose the kind of advertising claiming that a piece of merchandise is worth *more* than the price at which it is offered. I don't believe in comparative price advertising, and for two main reasons. It is devious. And, generally speaking, it is not believable.

Many years ago the company bearing my name laid down its final policy in this matter. The item we sell at 79¢ is a 79¢ item. We neither expect nor want customers of ours to think either that we are such poor business people as to believe we can sell them a $1 item for 79¢, or that we think them of such poor intelligence that they would actually think we could do so. One of our pleasures since the outset has been to educate our neighbors—our customers, if you prefer—in the values we give. Education by deeds, not by mere words. They must be better off for buying from us, and know why it is a fact.

People know instinctively that a merchant cannot afford to lose money on the goods he sells. To say nothing of being honest, advertising which carries a message of full value in exchange for every dime spent is clear evidence of business responsibility. I do not believe many customers think that a business can continue long in operation without reasonable profit. People have remarked to me that the stores of our company never seem to run many bargain sales. That is true. I do not believe either that people are very gullible about "bargains" or that so-called "bargain sales" are the way to build customer-confidence. Overly dramatic bargain sales raise questions in my mind. Is the merchant a poor buyer, seeking this quick escape from his own mistakes? Is he misrepresenting values in the "bargains"? Is he wooing customers, deliberately taking a loss in expectation of later making it up?

The company which uncompromisingly adheres to the practice of furnishing full value for the price advertised builds tremendous confidence for itself. When people know they will find no "catches" in your advertising or your goods, that they can believe to the letter everything you say, the business results will surely be good. To my mind public confidence in your business is the next thing to tangible. After our cornerstone of Golden Rule dealing, my personal opinion is that the next most important factor of our rock foundation of public confidence has been the steady avoidance of comparative price advertising. Coming from me that might at first glance seem a rather opinionated assertion but I take pride in our policy, even though responsible merchants whom I respect are sometimes inclined to disagree with my conviction.

In line with the principle that a straight line is the shortest distance between two points, I believe that customers are reached both quickly and permanently by direct, honest appeals to common sense and thrifty buying desires. I don't think they feel either comfortable or safe in a Never-Never land of fantasy values but that, on the contrary, goods and advertising which are offered in the Do-unto-others spirit will never lose but always gain for the merchant.

I have known many merchants who frankly did not believe it is "practical" business, to spend money on advertising which does not cite comparative prices. There seems to be a tendency to fear that an honest, straight-forward invitation to buy is not sufficiently strong; that unless there is a suggestion of "something for nothing" people will be reluctant to buy. So far as my experience goes, this reasoning is fallacious.

By comparison with 1960's sophisticated advertising copy standards, at the time I was keeping store in Kemmerer, Wyoming and for some years thereafter, certainly such advertising as I did was, as the phrase has it, "corny." We used handbills liberally and, both in these and my advertisements in the newspapers I made a point to *talk* with prospective customers, exactly as I would talk with them face-to-face in the store, or if I met them on the street. Whatever I said about the merchandise I had to sell was hard-hitting, enthusiastic, telling all about the goods, at the same time keeping it both honest and believable. It may seem a homemade formula but there must have been something to it, for that one small store grew into 1700 stores and very close to a billion-and-a-half-dollar business.

Today there is an ever-growing sound and healthy relationship between advertising and doing business. Media—newspapers, magazines, radio, TV—are the marketplace, where business can cry its wares. Media afford the opportunity and forms for bringing to the notice of the public the advantages of buying what is for sale. It is advertising which enables media to prosper, at the same time being able to afford to bring readers interesting and informative reading other than advertising news. There is a mutuality of interest, working to the benefit of all concerned; to business advertisers, to proprietors of media, to the general public which reads, listens and views.

Advertising is an economical as well as energizing element of business. It is almost ludicrous to mention the plight which would overtake any merchant if he could only advertise what he had to sell by individually sending an advertisement daily to every home in town. The cost of trying individually to get a message into every home which would be equivalent to the message carried by the newspaper or other media would be staggering; indeed its cost to the advertiser would unquestionably exceed the gross business that would result from it. Even if a merchant were courageous enough to attempt such a method, from the speed with which the waste basket receives the bulk of circulars and other "uninvited guests" arriving in our mail, it is clear that such do-it-yourself tactics would completely fail.

It has been very interesting to me to see the practice of advertising grow from the purely local to a national and indeed international instrument for expanding business. The basic mission of advertising, whatever form it takes, is to spread news, mainly commercial news. As business and industry have expanded, such "commercial" news has frequently become news in the journalistic sense as well. For example, the announcement of a new Ford car, an IBM computer, a new type of aircraft for commercal aviation. Increasingly women—who in the main handle the budget and do the family purchasing —cannot wait to get the paper, to find out the latest news as to production of articles they need to buy. And men and women alike will say that they read the newspapers and magazines as much for the advertisements as for articles and other editorial content.

I would not want to leave this subject—which, as a merchant, I believe touches a vital part of our everyday living—without testifying emphatically to my conviction that, in the eyes of those who read and following advertising and advertisements, the messages conveyed by advertisements *are*, in effect, the institutions behind them. The obligation is therefore clear. There is no substitute for honesty in the news conveyed. Exaggerations of values, slick shadings of quality, facile wording which confuses rather than engendering confidence—these betray the public goodwill and hurt the cause of Business. When the merchant's principles and policies of doing business are right and consistent, he will be known for selling goods, and those only, which are the best value for the money; when his attitude of service stands back of his attitude as to value, truthful advertising will bring him all the customers he can serve.

The practice of advertising is growing in conscience and ethical standards. I noticed with great satisfaction a recent story in the newspapers about a "ready reference" compilation got out by the Association of National Advertisers, pertaining to "basic criteria between honest and lawful advertising, and misleading and deceptive, hence unlawful, advertising." Though the point was recognized that "Advertising, like the creative art it employs, is inseparable from drama, illusion and the selective readjustment of reality which is the essence of artistic functions . . ." it was emphasized that "Illusion may not become delusion." This is a strong step in the right direction and could accomplish the disappearance of many faults.

If I may allow myself a small departure at this point from the serious to the less serious, I should like to share with the reader a small anecdote which came to my attention through the entertainer, Art Linkletter, in *The Secret World of Kids*. I like to think of it, in its way, as a testimonial to our usefulness in the community.

It seems that one day, in that portion of his daytime TV program devoted by Linkletter to allowing children to speak their minds on subjects that interest them, a boy of about six or seven years was excited at the moment about something that happened to Adam and Eve. He explained animatedly that they lived in the Garden of Eden, didn't have to wear clothes, and liked to eat apples. One day they were disobedient, he said, and got put out of the garden for it.

"But if they didn't wear any clothes—" inquired Mr. Linkletter.

"Oh," he was assured, "they went to J. C. Penney's and bought some."

CHAPTER XVII

Individual and Community Self-Reliance

Earlier I mentioned certain boyhood object lessons in self-reliance. My father's views on encouraging self-reliance in the young was no narrow one. He was a student of American history, and saw self-reliance as a typical American quality which had played an important part in and characterized our amazing development as a nation.

I am interested in self-reliance for both individuals and for communities. In fact, between the mounting degree to which government is getting into community affairs which should be autonomous, and some tendency of individuals to rely on various welfare-state devices rather than their own efforts, I am more than ever interested in the development of individual self-reliance as a step toward its best flowering, namely, community self-reliance which, after all, simply consists in individual self-reliant action rendered in the organized framework of the community.

In boyhood years I had several experiences which taught me that, paradoxically, it is possible to be too self-reliant. In looking after my own interests, I stepped on interests of others. Later on I had lessons which, though of a somewhat different kind, were equally hard, which showed me the barrenness of self-reliance which leaves out God.

Not long ago I heard of the formidable pattern of living laid out for herself by a young woman who is determined to make her life self-reliant, to offset certain exceptional advantages which she inherited rather than earning them for herself. She is entering her thirties, is an excellent mother to three children, is unusually beautiful, and has great wealth. Besides actively running her home and caring for her family, she has a professional career, and also is consistently active with several important philanthropic interests. Obviously she has organized her life with efficiency and serious consideration for that obligation which all of us have, namely, "to pull our weight" as responsible human beings. I am sure that many of the things she has chosen to make up her life afford her concrete satisfaction. To my mind she illustrates a fact of life, namely, that self-interest is not necessarily opposed to the general good, but rather bound up with it.

I have cited this instance because it furnishes an example of both self-reliance and self-interest which can readily be emulated on their own terms by all young people.

I believe we are born with the instinct to help. For this reason, tremendous responsibility rests with parents, to inculcate ideas of service in their children, to adjust the perspective of children and young people as they go along to the outlets for service. It should not sound strange if I say that I feel some understanding of the juvenile delinquent. He or she is at a stage of development when energy and ideas of helping and doing are bursting. If parental sympathy and understanding guidance are lacking, sheer momentum may carry them easily in wrong directions and soon, they may find themselves wound up in situations which in one sense are really of parental making.

One reason I am so continually impressed with what the country owes to groups such as the Boy Scouts and Girl Scouts, the Campfire Girls, the Masons-affiliated Order of De Molay, which teaches young men ranging in ages from 14 to 21 years "clean and upright living by inculcating and practicing the virtues of comradeship, reverence, love of parents, patriotism, courtesy, cleanness and fidelity," the Future Farmers of America, the 4-H clubs, and the Young Men's and Young Women's Christian Associations, is that all of them teach young people self-reliance, in terms of character and the capacity for leadership.

Young people who are themselves self-reliant will have a natural interest and pride in helping to make their communities self-reliant.

Not long ago I heard of an incident in a small community which perfectly illustrates community progress through self-reliance. Literally everybody in the community, from children six and seven years old to the oldest inhabitants among a population of three hundred, contributed something. The incident centered around a need for a new schoolhouse.

The existing building was a delapidated nuisance over a hundred years old. For a generation everyone had recognized the need for a new one—unanimously insisting, however, that the town couldn't stand the rise in taxes necessary to get it.

Three public-spirited citizens (taxpayers) "got up on their

hind legs," as rebellion is phrased in that section of the country. They devised what they believed was a workable plan to get the school within the limitations. First and foremost among the limitations was holding the tax rate down; also, the town's borrowing power would have to suffice.

A site was selected and its owner donated it. A civil engineer did the surveying as his contribution to the community. An architect drew plans as his.

State government officials came on the run with offers of assistance, under certain supervisory conditions, of course. "Thanks just the same," said the Town committee, "we figgered out the way to do this without outside aid."

Small fry, and Girl and Boy Scouts helped clear the land, with adults overseeing "brush parties" through several weekends. A subscription list went around, to supplement the town's borrowing power of $12,000 not only with voluntary contributions in money, but pledges of materials and day labor. A woodcutter, for example, contributed three days' labor of assembling small lumber; a carpenter made window casings, a glazier contributed glass, cut and installed it. A young man, a brilliant concert pianist, who had come many summers as a camper to the boys' camp at the head of the lake, came down from his native Montreal and gave a concert in the village church as his contribution to the school building fund. Townswomen hooked rugs and sold them, contributing the proceeds. And so it went. You could hardly look over the tax list and pick out the name of one person who didn't contribute in some way.

The new school building, designed so knowingly that no "population explosion" for the next hundred years will render it obsolete, was "brought in", as they say in the motion picture industry and the oil fields, for a sum in the neighborhood of $25,000—with a rise of no more than $2.00 in taxes to anyone in town, thanks to cooperative action.

This is of course not the only example of the general kind over the country, but it is a dramatic reminder that community self-reliance has by no means gone out of fashion; ingrained in the true American way of life, it has a way of asserting itself when really needed.

Several years ago I had the opportunity to make a trip around the world by plane. Through talking with leaders of many governments, and of business and agriculture, I received valuable insight and understanding; in return I offered some experiences of my own with the power of Christian principles in business and the democratic way of life. In many places I was particularly struck with the manifest desire of the people to be self-reliant. They valued proofs of our friendship, in economic aid along lines of technical assistance, and —even more so, I gathered—opportunities to learn from our economic and other "know how." Yet, it seemed to me, their main and deep wish—as individuals, and collectively for their country in the concert of nations—remained to learn, as rapidly as possible, *to do for themselves*. It strengthened a conviction I have long held, namely that self-reliance is not an "acquired taste," but generally so fundamental a longing that it is really a part of what we call "human nature" itself.

Our American way of life is so constituted as to renew itself constantly from within, but we must remember that the renewal will not be automatic. Real effort on the part of all is constantly necessary in order to preserve and expand it. Business leaders, like those in other areas of thought and action, have a great responsibility in this vital movement. How well are we doing our part beyond making our individual business successful and safe?

Some of us ask ourselves how far government can be allowed to get into business. But I think we must ask ourselves also how much we have neglected, leaving it for others to do, perhaps inadvertently, through a lazy attitude toward the need and animating strength of self-reliance, in its widest meaning.

Washington cannot do the job alone and, of course, should not. In fact, many government leaders stress the need for citizens to organize their communities to a greater interest in economics, and to take cooperative responsible action for many projects which properly can be taken care of locally. From the economic standpoint, by lowering costs, and lessening demands on government funds self-reliant action is efficient and provident. From the spiritual standpoint the creative potential of the people involved has opportunity, individually and collectively, to compete *affirmatively* on solutions of problems common to society, hence in the interest of all. Here again is an indication that self-interest and the general good are bound together, here again it pays to be selfish—unselfishly. Aggressive action growing out of the combining of unselfish individual service, the spirit of citizen responsibility and the will to collective self-reliance will give tremendous forward motion to our American way of life, in the very terms in which it came into being. Most of us today are thinking in terms of both national and international developments. We need and want a strong nation—spiritually, physically, militarily and economically; but we can have a strong nation only with the active participation of the people in their relationships within the states and local communities. To get the people to take informed and aggressive action is the way to establish unity. Our own self-interest is dependent ultimately upon all-out, aggressive movement that encourages individual initiative, citizen responsibility, and community self-reliance. It may not safely be left to chance. Millions of people are likely to lose their courage and slip backward at the first encounter with dislocation. The tendency in threatening circumstances is to turn for rescue to the federal government, neither a good nor a historically American measure.

Aggressively self-reliant communities can shed the light of example. To suggest an illustration; I have mentioned how one tiny community—rather like a young, fearless terrier seizing and subduing an enemy—seized and conquered its schoolhouse problem. Hundreds of communities throughout the land need the benefit of better schoolhouses; few are so situated that, by any stretch of resolve, ingenuity, collective action and combination of borrowing power, cash subscriptions and voluntary labor, they could get what is needed for $25,000. But many could take inspiration and find ways to adapt to scale the example of this tiny community. What can never be reckoned in dollars is the pride of a community in such exercise of the will to self-reliance.

The American people, working together in their classic tradition can reach great heights of community self-reliance.

It has long seemed to me that encouragement of greater self-reliance and community responsibility in government, and the systematic fostering and coordination of those forces which give vitality and rich meaning to community life are among the best hopes of our freedom and independence. A certain amount of bureaucratic government is necessary in the functioning of a nation such as ours but we should never lose sight of the fact that *voluntary* cooperation for community self-reliance is the most effective cooperation, for when the people of a community determine their own activities for which they choose their own leaders, they have something which is their *very* own, something that direct interest and the spirit of service can animate. In its way it is rather like the large, abstract company structure, and the type of business wherein, when a man begins to get responsibility, he can feel that he is really in business for himself.

Self-reliance, individual and collective, is very much like a business which is based on right principles, where what benefits one, benefits all.

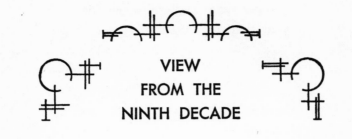

VIEW
FROM THE
NINTH DECADE

CHAPTER XVIII

The Spirit and Practice of Brotherhood

By nature I am prone to appraise situations in the light of favoring signs. In thinking about our responsibility in the problem of true brotherhood in the world, I see clearly that we have every resource and incentive with which to advance its spirit and practice among men—and are not working hard enough at it. Our attention to it comes and goes. We take for granted the "frailty of human nature," shrugging off suspicion, doubt, fear, resentment and envy that are holding men far apart. We are part of a civilization capable of most marvelous scientific, industrial and other advances yet, by comparison with our progress in material fields, we have scarcely made a beginning in the art of brotherhood. In Fyodor Dostoevsky's *The Brothers Karamazov* a character says, "Until you have become really, in actual fact, a brother to everyone, brotherhood will not come to pass."

Several years ago the great photographer, Edward Steichen,

arranged an exhibition of 503 pictures from 68 countries for the Museum of Modern Art. He titled it "The Family of Man." The title stays with me. *The Family of Man*—does it not express the essence of brotherhood?

Each has his own image of the brotherhood of man, and of the forms by which it is best expressed. We agree intellectually with the definition that "the salvation of society, the hope for the free, full development of humanity, is in the gospel of brotherhood, the gospel of Christ." Many centuries ago, when another civilization was pressing terrible inequities, there arose an unschooled carpenter to preach the gospel of the fatherhood of God, the equality and brotherhood of men; he taught his disciples to pray for the coming of the Kingdom of Heaven on earth. Ever since the idea has risen and fallen like the tides, rising and falling in cadence with men's concern for the idea, the ideal, of a common brotherhood. Can we think about this as one of the sacred trusts of our times and, each in his own way, according to his own image of brotherhood, begin to make up for lost time?

It will not be easy. Not for lack of good intention but because, being wrapped up in our own affairs, we are rather like those bidden to the marriage feast; "And they all with one consent began to make excuse. . . ."

One of our readiest excuses is our consciousness of things which cause people to be different from one another, things such as geographical locations and boundaries, racial origins and strains, language, religions, customs, even foods. The differences have old, tough roots and are not to be ignored.

It seems to me we are at a point when we should re-examine and strengthen our faith in His laws of love; our daily news-

papers leave no room to doubt that we are confronted with
that conflict in the world between the forces of good and evil
which the Bible describes as Armageddon.

Next to our trust in God Himself, our most important
article of faith is embodied in the spirit of true brotherhood.
Should we not, therefore, ask ourselves what constitutes that
spirit, and understand a few of the ways, at least, in which
we can apply it, in our own human relationships with the
world around us?

The first constituent of the true brotherhood spirit is, of
course, love for one's fellows. "Thou shalt love thy neighbor
as thyself." The word love has a variety of meanings. Good
will, strong liking, strong personal attachment growing out
of sympathetic understanding or ties of kinship, these are
among them.

To love our fellow beings presupposes certain expressed attitudes. Unselfishness, for example. "It is more blessed to give
than to receive," Christ said. One wishes to be the kind of
person for whom this will be true materially as well as spiritually. If I may interject a personal note, it seems to me I only
began to learn spiritual giving after I saw that it must be put
second to getting.

The Apostle Paul wrote, "Love is the fulfilling of the law."
There is a deep, rich meaning there, I believe. He was speaking
at a time when men were "working their passage to Heaven,"
so to speak, by trying to keep the Ten Commandments and
those scores of supplemental commandments which, one
might say, became a problem in moral long-division.

Christ drew their attention to a more simple yet inclusive
standard for human conduct. If they would really love God

and their fellow beings, they would then be strengthened to fulfill the whole law, and religion would need no supporting legalistic machinery.

How often do we excuse ourselves by saying, "It is not easy to develop a feeling of love for all people"? Of course it is not, yet that is what is called for by the true brotherhood spirit.

Most of us need, first of all, much more understanding and patience than we possess in our dealings with other individuals. It is not hard to understand why we have difficulty in loving those who act in unkind or cruel ways for, in the human make-up, there is an innate protective instinct toward the hurt and suffering. We have an innate sense of resentment toward displays of selfishness, greed, ruthlessness and outright wickedness. We turn away, when we should be concerned to "overcome evil with good," trying to understand, find the good, and influence a mending of ways.

Never did the world call more insistently on us to exemplify that motivation of love which is seeking the fundamental ties that can bind different peoples together in mutual understanding, respect and appreciation, and in joining activity for a common purpose. All of us are prone to keep in mind the attitudes and attributes which single out people, rather than those qualities and talents which offer a basis of common sympathy and interest. We have all had the experience of making up our minds in advance that certain individuals or groups would not interest us at all, only to discover, on going through the motions of politeness in meeting them, that they were of great and rewarding interest indeed to us. The spirit of brotherhood in the world has suffered sadly from preconceived notions! And what could be more wasteful?

What I want to emphasize is our opportunities for looking

for fundamental similarities and areas for agreement. It goes without saying, when we find them, we have a firm basis for understanding, friendship and cooperative effort in directions which will be mutually desirable and beneficial.

Some of the bitterest conflicts in the history of mankind have revolved around religion. And yet should we not examine in the light of that the fact that the importance of loving one's neighbors is emphasized in each one of the major religions, besides being especially stressed in many parts of the New Testament? If sufficient efforts had been made in directions toward understanding, basic agreement and friendship, many destructive struggles could very likely have been avoided. Must we not ask ourselves, Why not still make them? Is there any more effective instrument for making them than the Golden Rule?

We are wont to propagandize the extent to which scientific advances in recent years, both in communications and transportation, have "made the world smaller," bringing the peoples of the world closer together. We pore over the marvels of jet flight, marveling that we can breakfast in New York and have dinner in London; and that yesterday when we had occasion to talk by telephone to a friend in Capetown, it couldn't have been easier to hear him if he had been at a desk on the floor below in the same building with us. But do we ask ourselves how this bringing of people "nearer" to us has increased the need—call it, rather, the opportunity—to apply more creative and understanding attitudes of mind to the resultant associations? Have not nuclear weapons of surpassing destructive potential become an ever-present symbol of the tremendous vigilance we must concentrate on offsetting the dangers by building a more convincing harmony of interests?

It is hard to see how we can justify fearful weapons from the standpoint of religious thinking. From the standpoint of preparedness against possible attack, and the preservation of our chosen tradition of liberty, we know from the scientists that there is no technological defense of much effectiveness against atomic and hydrogen bombs. Many of our leading scientists find themselves in abject terror when they contemplate the threat to all mankind which, perforce, they have had to have a hand in creating.

Several years ago in *Foundation for Reconstruction*, Dr. Elton Trueblood, Professor of Philosophy at Earlham College and religious director of the U.S. Information Service, said emphatically and quite realistically, I think, that the only answer there ever could be to atomic power is moral power. This force is, of course, readily identifiable with the spirit of true brotherhood, rooted in love.

I would not want to be thought a visionary or idealistic dreamer, for I believe that, actually, I am very much the realist. Should our country again find itself forced to defend itself against attack, I would count myself among the vast majority of freedom-loving Americans who would again give every possible support, material and spiritual, to stop aggression.

Now few of us have the opportunity to serve on committees of the United Nations, and relatively few in the structure for making our laws. But that certainly does not prevent us "being members one of another" in forwarding the Gospel of Love, through our everyday relationships.

Her faults and shortcomings notwithstanding, America stands today as the greatest nation in the world. But can we say we are as solvent spiritually as we are materially? We ought to be, for we are possessed of a tremendous wealth in what we may call spiritual assets. Back of us lies a history of more than three centuries of freedom of religion, and of democracy. Our country stands as evidence that upon these foundation stones an efficient, strong society can rise.

A number of times in the course of this book, I have spoken of the role of the individual in the advancement of our ideals in all ways, secular as well as spiritual. We are part of the Family of Man and must pray for larger understanding and creative sympathy in hard situations around the world. For example, great numbers of people in the world today are being sorely tried because, in dangerous proximity to Communism and other ideological threats, *they* want to be, and to continue as, Christians. They greatly need bolsters to their courage and faith to hold fast. We have opportunity as individuals to proffer reassurance in their Christian allegiance.

I would not exactly call myself what often is labeled a "joiner" in the sense of belonging to a great many organizations or groups for the reason that, by some standard, it seems the thing to do. The organizations I have become associated with have certain characteristics in common. I became a Mason at a time when I was in dire spiritual need, and Masonry is based on the Bible. It does not imply a substitute for religion. It is religious because its principles are Christian principles.

My reason for association with Rotary is connected with its aims. The motto of Rotary is "He profits most who serves best; Service above Self." I am impressed too with the Kiwanis aim, expressed powerfully in two words, "We build."

Could there be any more concise enunciation of the essence of brotherhood than these?

John Wesley had a rule, and it was a good one; it seems to me that the aspiration to chart all business and other human dealings by Christian principles squares with it.

> Do all the good you can;
> By all the means you can;
> In all the ways you can;
> To all the people you can;
> As long as ever you can.

Think about it. Does it not square too with the spirit and practice of brotherhood?

I should like to share my appreciation for a statement * on this subject made not long ago by Archbishop William L. Wright, Grand Master Royal Arch Masons of Canada. Describing the purpose of the fraternity, he said:

> There is nothing that this world needs now more than the making of friends among men . . . a focus of fellowship in which men may be brought together, to know and understand, and therefore love, each other. It is our desire to make friends of men in the world; bring men a little closer together so that each may feel the heartbeat of the other, sit down together, and learn to be friends . . . Underneath all the sectarianism of the modern time, and in spite of iron, and bamboo curtains, men want to be friends . . . If we knew what is going on in the hearts of men, we would discover that their deep hunger is for a greater friendship for each other. This friendship must be centered in God. It is because this principle has been repudiated that there are tensions in the world scene. A man's first duty is to God. He must

* *The Royal Arch Mason.* Issued under the direction of the General Grand Chapter, Royal Arch Masons.

worship Him, serve Him, love Him with all his heart, mind, soul and strength . . . Keep this thought uppermost in all life and thinking . . . It may be possible to possess all the temporal assets a society can produce, but if the character of man is not sufficiently stable to handle these mundane weapons, he may lack the one thing needful to give significance to his eternal destiny which is, belief in and surrender to the Great Architect of the Universe.

VIEW
FROM THE
NINTH DECADE

CHAPTER XIX

Not Retirement But Change of Activity

I never think of myself as retired. The main reason is that I'm not worked out. I am sufficiently busy for it to take a bit of arranging if I am to get to the opera Monday nights during the season.

When I waked up one recent morning I was in the midst of dreaming that I was selling a pair of plain, serviceable shoes to a customer back in Kemmerer for $2.98. I was convincing her that she might find shoes elsewhere for $1 less, but these would give her better service because they were better shoes than $1.98 could possibly buy.

Except occasionally at some store opening or a Founder's Day I don't often sell shoes any more. But I like knowing that I can, if opportunity arises.

Nevertheless, we all recognize retirement as a subject which students of social problems are taking very seriously. I take it seriously myself, though perhaps not for the same reasons as some others. To me the word retirement hints at inactivity, a slackening hold on the reins of living. In that sense, I don't believe in retirement. I do most certainly believe in *a change of activity*, when it becomes time for what is commonly called retirement. I like very much a point made by Dr. Harry Emerson Fosdick: "The art of retirement is not only to retire from something, but to retire to something." In my case I can see little difference between activities of my ninth decade and the evolving ones of the seven preceding decades; they are just arranged differently.

I began thinking a long time ago about problems of older people and quite specifically as long ago as 1926 when, as a memorial to my parents, I established a Home Community, so-named, for retired ministers and their wives. If I here sketch in its purpose and functioning briefly I do so because it seems to me to approach elements of human living in a way to *conserve*, so to speak, instead of *shelving*.

I took the opportunity of providing for such a community from the standpoint of having first-hand knowledge that, whereas almost universally ministers and their families lead lives of dedication and sharp sacrifice, the material rewards are woefully lacking, hardly admitting even the smallest financial provision for the declining years; when through with the work in which many a minister and his wife have served faithfully for a lifetime, they find themselves not only without material resources to see them through, but cut off, as well, from activities which would keep spirits and morale intact. I cannot say too strongly, we should not reward people as indispensable as these with only cause for anxiety.

I resolved to make the Memorial Home Community one place, among what I hoped might become many, where such men and their helpmeets could face the future with inner quiet.

Twenty-three simple, comfortable houses are arranged, in general casually, as they might be in a French village. Each house has three to four pleasant apartments, completely equipped and furnished. Several acres of garden give anyone with the impulse an invitation to dig in soil, and to spend time in the sunshine. A number and variety of activities go on as a matter of course; book review, and discussion, groups; golf tournaments on the community's own 9-hole course; Red Cross projects, and mending of usable apparel to be sent to the needy overseas; nearby church activities to give residents added scope for the joy and satisfaction of keeping in touch with the calling in which their lives are rooted.

As I saw it this was the key to the whole thing, namely to surround our friends who came to live in the Home Community with a *continuity* of interest. People who have led full and active lives—and never let anyone tell you that at any time the life of the average minister and his wife is anything but full and active!—cannot, and should not, either be forced or expected to accept "retirement" in the sense of permanent hibernation. Nothing either inwardly satisfying or outwardly productive ever can come of that "resting" which becomes either mere puttering or induced inertia. Those who have amassed years of experience have stored up mature wisdom which can, and should, be of continuing value to the world. One of the most short-sighted, wasteful, downright destructive and incidentally cruel errors in our modern society is the putting of such people "out to pasture." Among those dealing with the whole problem, the most successful, individuals or group, are those giving thought and planning to helping people prepare *for active, productive later years.* Older people *can* be vital and therefore happy, consequently able while they live to continue contributing to the sum of human progress.

At the same time that ground was broken for the Home Community, in June of 1926, the cornerstone of the Penney Memorial Chapel was laid. My associate in certain enterprises, Ralph W. Gwinn (who was a partner in the firm of our legal counsel until he entered politics and became the Republican representative in Congress of the 27th New York District) gave to the chapel a memorial to his own mother, in the form of a beautiful pipe organ; my two elder sons provided a memorial to their mother, Berta Hess Penney, in the form of a lovely screen leading from the body of the chapel into the community rooms, with her name lettered in gold on its door.

An inevitable aftermath of events experienced in connection with the Miami activities was that for some time my resources for furthering my various philanthropic interests were curtailed to almost nothing. The J. C. Penney Foundation headquarters were moved over to the offices of CHRISTIAN HERALD, on Fourth Avenue. I wanted exceedingly that none of the Foundation facets should have to go out of existence for lack of necessary support, thus we retrenched wherever we could. More and more I saw how ideal it would be if the several objectives could, administratively, be welded into one CHRISTIAN HERALD complex, embracing work for children (Montlawn Vacation Centre for underprivileged children), for overseas missions (Industrial School and Orphanages in Foochow, China), for the rescue mission (Bowery Mission in New York), and for retired ministers (Memorial Home Community), all placed in the guiding hands of Dr. Poling who long since had to me evidenced his superlative

powers. I turned over intact to him the CHRISTIAN HER-
ALD—I had resigned from its presidency and, later from the
Board—and subsequently put the Memorial Home Community in his charge, although I remained on its Board because of
my intimate personal relationship to its purposes.

As I knew they would in Dr. Poling's hands, the changes
effected worked for good. By 1933 the CHRISTIAN HER-
ALD, which had experienced some rough sledding, was safely
in the black. In time it built an apartment building of approximately 100 apartments on the Home Community grounds, to
take care of the individual resident as other houses provided
for couples.

However happy our experience with fruition of the Memorial Home Community plan, of course it is a fact that the
problem of human retirement poses many differing problems
calling for many differing solutions.

For a different kind of example, not long ago I received a
letter from a man who had retired after being with our company since 1917. Some things he said may increase the thoughtful reader's insight into the nature of readjustments that enter
in, and for that reason I should like to sketch them in.

One part of his letter holding a particular interest for me
personally, though it had nothing to do per se with his retirement, was the statement that he came to us for a starting salary of $60.00 though he had been receiving $150.00 in a bank.
I have said elsewhere in this book that we were constantly on
the lookout for men with the vision and adventurous courage
to make temporary sacrifices, if necessary in terms of money,
in exchange for opportunity.

"I remember to this day," this man wrote, "the look of surprise that came over the face of Mr. J—— in the bank when I told him I had accepted a position with the Golden Rule (at that time our store was still known by that name) for $60.00, and he just came right out and told me what a fool he thought I was. Fourteen years later, when I happened to be in his city, I went to call on him. His advancement had been less than mine, and he made it a point to tell me how foolish he had been in expressing himself to me as he did."

I interject this because it emphasizes the soundness of the idea that the kind of men we wanted with us would be men who could grasp the idea of placing opportunity first.

Apropos of his retirement experience, he wrote, "It is not an easy thing to bring one's habits to an abrupt stop, and I am sure that I shall miss coming down to the store each morning and going through the various departments, opening the mail and sharing in the excitement of the new merchandise that comes in each day. *I am* glad that I have interests that will take up most of my time, and I plan to keep busy as long as I have my health. I think of you with your keen interest in the Company, and what it has meant to you to keep your forward-looking approach to life. Certainly it has had much to do with preserving your vitality and keenness of perception. . . .

"I believe that my years with our Company have given me (besides material rewards) a real opportunity to serve my fellow man with the God-given abilities that are mine. One never uses these abilities to the fullest, but the important thing is that the opportunity is there, day after day. . . ."

Some years ago the H.C.S.C. (Honor, Confidence, Service, Cooperation) Club of the Penney Company devised a pamph-

let furnishing a sort of course in "preparation for retirement."
I know that some other companies have done approximately
the same thing, and wish more might. There is a distinct
service to be rendered prospective retire-ees, giving them an
insight into some aspects to be expected of the transition
period between employment and retirement, and a better
understanding of what retirement can be made to mean.

The H.C.S.C. Club Inc. began printing in January of 1953
regular issues of a paper named *The Inventory Sheet*. For its
first printed issue I set down five suggestions for a vigorous
and rewarding life after retirement; it seemed to me that,
among other things, their emphasis was on being a good
American.

1. To build yourself a program of activities—social, political,
humanitarian, recreational—for a full and well-balanced life.

2. Stick to that program!

3. Enjoy the satisfaction of helping others.

4. Don't rest on your laurels financially; use some of your
time to produce income, however little; Penney men should
continue to meet that challenge, too.

5. Have faith in God and in the power of prayer, not only
on Sundays, but every day, every hour.

I should like to think that every retired person was devoting
a regular share of time to the job of being a good American,
by actively being a good citizen. There is more to being a
good citizen than just going to the polls on election day.
There is work to be done in literally every community, and
to help in doing it is, among other things, making a return
on benefits we receive through living in this great country.
That we are often remiss in making this return was brought
home to me when I read some disheartening figures, in the

American Agriculturalist, on the lack of interest of average citizens in how their government is being run. One township, with 683 registered voters, had only 40 registered for one's year's primaries which, as it happened, were vitally important. In another village, an open meeting of the Board of Education brought out only six people including the three-man school board, and this was a meeting at which a $31,154 budget was adopted!

Where are we when we should be making it our business to participate in matters of importance to everyone?

With respect to retirement of Penney men, I often reflect that, if each one would make good citizenship his continuing business, how much could be accomplished in helping to restore freedom to Free Enterprise, and America to its God-given heritage.

Like the Golden Rule, retirement will really work—if we make it. Many people do have a psychological fear of retirement; they have a fear of not knowing what to do with time, a fear of dilapidating mentally "with nothing to do," a fear that the only proof that one is alive will seem to be that one is walking around.

I am sure that one great bulwark against these ghostly fears is preparation. Some years ago a retired manager said, regretfully, "If I had this thing to do all over again, I would spend a good part of my last year developing things to do to avoid the deadly vacuum in which I now find myself." Others, practically from the first hour of retirement, lay out such a program of satisfying and useful activity that they simply never get around to being at loose ends.

Capacity for work will vary with the individual, at age 60, 70, 80. It is unlikely that the man of 60 will be able to perform at that age in the same manner as in his youth; yet we all know of men who are able to accomplish as much as in their youth, though it will be at a slower pace. However, it is well to remember that a sudden and complete shut-down can become as disastrous as overdoing. I recall a man whose retirement was looming; he felt distressed by the prospect and went to his physician for a check-up. He plied the doctor with questions as to how much he could continue to do, how much his condition of health would oblige him to slow down. The doctor's advice was wise. "Just act your age," he said. That made it easier for the man who, being a person of common sense, had a reasonable judgment as to what he could and could not, or should not, do.

Aside from the overall "Not retirement, try instead a change of activity," my formula for retirement for myself can hardly be said to be a formula at all. I have no interest in counting up but would say, offhand, that I continue to travel about the same number of thousands of miles each year as usual. I leave management's provinces and prerogatives to management but the calendar has not notified me to stop being interested in the business; I continue to be a director, and regularly attend directors' meetings. I make a great many store visits, and speak when I am invited to do so. Each spring I spend several weeks at the farms in Missouri; I am as interested in the herd developments as I was when we had only Emmadine in 1922. And nothing refreshes me more than taking time to walk around the farms and just reflect; then I am at the natural source of the influences and ideals that have most influenced my whole life. However complex life becomes, "in the beginning God created the heaven and the earth."

Do not misunderstand me. I see no worth in dwelling on

the past for the sake of dwelling on it. I see retirement rather as a sort of dividend, with which to open up new avenues of activity, to fill days with pleasant occupation for ourselves and possible service to others. Creatively accepted, retirement does not narrow horizons, it widens them. For each of us there is some opportunity, to put at the service of our fellows the wisdom accumulated through experience.

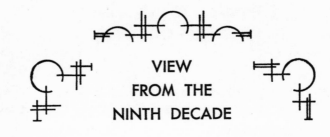

VIEW FROM THE NINTH DECADE

CHAPTER XX

View from the Ninth Decade

During a store visit I observed a tall, rawboned man making his way toward me with some determination. He looked to me like an old-style rancher. "You are Mr. J. C. Penney, are you?" he said quietly, thrusting out a hand that had done a lot of hard work; he looked keenly down at me with appraising steel-gray eyes. When I said I was, he went on, "Well, I just thought I'd see what it's like to shake hands with a millionaire."

Taken aback, I said, "My friend, I'm pleased that you came into our store. I wish, though, that it was a Christian you wanted to shake hands with instead of a millionaire." I am not quite sure that he believed me. Perhaps after he thought it over, though, he would understand that it is more important to be recognized as a Christian than as a millionaire.

Early in my career I came and applied at one of the large banks in New York City to establish a line of credit. The number of stores and the company were growing, and we needed the greater efficiency of setting up our buying and accounting offices close to our sources of supply. I had my financial statement to show the president of the bank, and told him our cost of doing business. I explained our fixed, unchangeable policy of doing business by the Golden Rule, and the working of our partnership profit-sharing plan whereby I trained a man to run a store as manager, who then trained another man to run another store, and so on, in a chain of men linked by a self-renewing idea.

"Your partnership plan is interesting, all right," he observed finally. "The trouble with it is that it won't work."

I knew then that he was mistaken and I know it now even better, after nearly sixty years of merchandising experience. Sincerely practiced the Golden Rule simply cannot fail to work.

I wanted as a boy to grow up and be a success. So I am in sympathy, to start with, with the thousands of young people I meet in the course of a year, whose minds are fixed on achieving success. Some of them are worried. They have heard the false prophets, saying that the time of the individual and free enterprise is gone. As I have by no means ceased to be a merchant in terms of practical thinking, I can assure them, on the basis of what I have learned and am still learning from experience, that if they will place their trust and reliance on the practicability of Christian principles, they will find success. I don't limit the term—and hope they won't—to money. Money is a form of success but it is not all of it.

There are people, of course, who see it as naive and old fashioned to plead the preparatory effect of the solidarity of home and family on the only kind of success worth having—the kind which analyzes according to the Golden Rule. If the great basic principles are old fashioned, then I say thank God for it.

Charles Steinmetz, the late great engineer at General Electric, once made a disclosure to a newspaper interviewer which conveys a significant point. Discussing his career, Steinmetz said, "I have had no plan or blueprint. As a young man, I only wanted to be a success, *and that is no plan*. Foolishly, as a boy I wished the curtain of life could be lifted so I could see the future. How glad I am that it couldn't—for I might have missed the rewards of curiosity. You ask what I mean. Well, aren't scientific discoveries and advances all, in essence, rewards of curiosity?"

Though I most certainly cannot claim to have been thinking along the same line when I started out, I think I might now almost regard what I have learned through experience about the workability of Christian principles in competitive business as a form of "rewards of curiosity." Like the banker who believed our plan wasn't workable, all along the way people assured me freely that it was visionary and unrealistic to rely on high-sounding principles for anything as realistically concrete as success. However destructive the assurance, it had one constructive use. It challenged your curiosity. And so, on the basis of the "rewards" of finding out that principles most certainly will work in a hard, practical world, I have no hesitancy about assuring young people who ply me with requests for the secrets of success, that so far as I know the only "secret"—actually no secret at all—is to give principles a chance to show what they can do and they, in turn, will point the way to opportunity to show what you can do.

When I talk with young people about the practicalities of pursuing success, as, happily, I am often asked to do, I rather like (hoping, of course to avoid the pitfall of seeming to "tell everybody what to do") to draw on Socrates' favorite method, which was "first to destroy preconceived notions, then point the way to truth, letting the student find his way for himself." One of the preconceived notions I must admit I relish doing my part to destroy is that the Golden Rule is, "Well, a nice ideal and aim but, in the practical sense, obsolete." Among the forms of success that have come to our company, operating by the Golden Rule principle through the partnership-profit sharing plan, are sales of more than a billion dollars, so perhaps I do not correctly understand the word obsolete! The returns in releasing the powers of men cannot be entered on the ledgers, of course, for they are incalculable.

For these and other reasons, I would have to stand by my belief that the "practicality" of applied principles appears in such working tools as right ambition, moral soundness, aboveboard dealings, self-discipline, hard work and normal intelligence. To my mind these, not genius, are the equipment required to achieve success. I believe the young people who sense this are in the majority. The schoolboy who asked me so eagerly to tell him how he could make a million dollars was not inherently a second-rate boy, I feel sure, but rather just young, still orienting himself in the qualities life asks, for what it has in store for us.

George Washington left us a thought which, at once, suggests a good beginning for those starting out, and for those who feel a responsibility to check position and correct performance along the way. "Labor to keep alive in your breast that little spark of celestial fire—your conscience," he bade us. In business as in all living, conscience and Christian principles are indivisible; we need only determine how far we are willing to apply them, in order to find success.

Asking myself how this book could be shaped to make it of modest usefulness, somewhat more practical than mere reminiscence, I recalled a legend which I like.

A man, journeying by chance through unfamiliar forest country, found his path interrupted by a narrow but deep ravine. He would get on, farther and faster, if he went down one side and up the other.

Instead he stopped to construct a small bridge, a rude bridge but strong and safe.

As he was finishing it another traveler, coming up with him, seeing his hard work yet surmising that he would not be passing this way a second time, said, "Why are you throwing away your strength on a bridge you will not use again?"

"Hark," replied the builder, cupping his ear to listen, "are not those the footfalls of younger men that we hear, coming from afar?"